# AGAK AGAK

For my father-in-law, Chris Denley (1957–2023),
whose bottomless appetite for food and life
will continue to inspire me.

# AGAK

Hardie Grant
BOOKS

# HOW WE EAT IN SINGAPORE

## (HOW TO USE THIS BOOK)

I've written this book in a way that mirrors how we eat in Singapore and how I still love to eat today.

### MOST DAYS, WE HAVE RICE AND THINGS THAT GO WITH RICE.

This is how we eat most often at home. Rice is the cornerstone of almost every meal, which is why I thought it would be most fitting to open the book with a chapter on rice. CHAPTER 1 contains simple and unembellished rice recipes, made for complementing recipes from CHAPTERS 2–5: CURRIES, BROTHS AND BRAISES, STIR-FRIES AND SIMPLE SIDES, FOOD FOR FEASTING. Pick one or two to make it a meal, or as many as you want for a full-blown dinner party.

### WE LIKE PICKY BITS BUT WE ALSO LOVE A DELICIOUS BOWLFUL.

CHAPTER 6 (One-Dish Meals) is full of those recipes that work by themselves, and no sides are necessary. It's the sort of food we have when we've got to fit in a quick lunch at the hawker centre; or here in the UK, when I want a comforting bowl to myself.

### WE FIND EVERY OPPORTUNITY FOR A TASTY TIDBIT.

Singaporeans love to snack and we'll make any excuse for a cheeky bite in between meals. You'll find salty, savoury, delightfully crunchy things in Little Bites (CHAPTER 7), then sweet puds, light cakes and cold refreshing treats in Sweet Things (CHAPTER 8).

### WE LOVE TO SPICE, SEASON AND SPRINKLE AWAY AT THE TABLE.

No, it's not rude to the cook to add a little extra to your own plate, and in fact you'll often find jars of sambal or tubs of pickles laid out on the table for people to help themselves to. Sauces and Sprinkles (CHAPTER 9) is filled with recipes for the extra bits, for both cooks and diners to add heat, crunch, fragrance or sharpness.

# CONTENTS

How We Eat in Singapore
(How to Use this book)  4

Introduction  9

Essential Singaporean Vocabulary  14

Essential Singaporean Pantry  16

## ONE

### Rice to Go with Everything

26

## TWO

### Curries

40

## THREE

### Broths and Braises

64

Alternative Contents  214

About the Author  216

Thank You  217

## FOUR
## Stir-fries and Simple Sides
82

## FIVE
## Food for Feasting
106

## SIX
## One-dish Meals
128

## SEVEN
## Little Bites
160

## EIGHT
## Sweet Things
180

## NINE
## Sauces and Sprinkles
200

# INTRODUCTION

**Agak is a Malay word meaning 'somewhat', and *agak agak*
is a colloquial term that loosely translates to 'estimate'.**

*Agak agak* doesn't exist only as a quirky, casual bit of Singlish. It's a way of thinking that comes to life in particular in the kitchen. A conversation with an Auntie in the family might go like this:

*'How much chilli and sugar for the achar?'*

*'Depends how hot the chilli is, lah. Sugar, you agak agak.
If you use more pineapple, you might want it less sweet.'*

That is not to say that every dish is a hot mess of random ideas and sheer luck. On the contrary, cooking the *agak agak* way is cooking with intent and intuition, honed by years of experience at the stove. In fact, while we have a special word for it, I would like to think *agak agak* is by no means exclusively Singaporean; it's an ability you'll recognise in good home cooks everywhere.

**Before I learnt how to cook, I learnt how
to taste, smell, touch and listen.**

I have never seen Mum use scales, nor measuring jugs. (The closest I have seen to her applying a vague sense of ratio to her cooking is when she uses the broken halves of eggshells to measure the amount of stock going into her steamed egg.) Instead, she relies on her senses – and a big dollop of common sense.

She knows to hold back on or add a pinch more salt, depending on how salty this new brand of soy sauce is. She can tell whether she needs to wet her hands with a tad more water if the dough for *mee hoon kueh* (handmade torn noodles) feels drier this time. This well of knowledge comes from a lifetime of trying and testing and tasting.

My earliest memories in my mum's kitchen weren't of me pounding *rempah* (spice paste) like a good little sous chef. In fact, like many Asian mums, she wanted me to focus on my homework/piano practice/extracurricular abacus classes ... anything but get her kitchen messy. But we were allowed to watch as she threw vegetables into the wok – the hard stalks first, the delicate leaves last. We were allowed to taste as she stirred together sauces from mysterious bottles and jars.

While it wasn't until many years later that I found my way in the kitchen, I picked up early on an appreciation for food – and an understanding of the tastes and textures that make food delicious.

**I learnt to cook Singaporean food in a London kitchen.**

I moved to London at the age of 18 and was forced to learn how to cook, through that same try-test-taste approach. Back then, London's food scene had yet to become the exciting, colourful hotpot it is today. I am still amazed that I can walk into Sainsbury's now and find fresh lemongrass among the bagged herbs on the shelves. In 2009, a craving for food from home meant a bus and two tube changes to Chinatown. So it became natural to make do with the ingredients I could easily get hold of. It didn't just make sense logistically, it made sense from a taste perspective, too.

Britain has a wonderful seasonal larder, bursting with fresh, vibrant produce. Instead of tamarind, I could choose to use sweet cherry tomatoes when I made a *sambal* in summer. Instead of hunting down long beans, I could stir-fry runner beans with *belacan* (fermented shrimp paste). Often, the results would be cheaper and taste better, as the ingredients hadn't been flown halfway across the world a week ago. It did mean that timings and ratios had to be adjusted and, without an exact recipe to instruct me, I had to be guided instead by my tastebuds and experience.

I used to hesitate to call some of these dishes 'Singaporean'. When I hosted supper clubs, I would often serve a traditional dish with an apologetic caveat that it's not exactly as you would find it in Singapore. And when I started my spice paste business, Rempapa Spice Co., I would worry that Singaporeans might miss the shrimp paste in our *sambal tumis*, as I had tweaked my recipe to be vegan-friendly to suit a wider audience. But it turned out that none of my diners nor customers found the food inauthentic. The Singaporeans living in London even confessed to having the same approach to cooking here. It warmed my heart to see Londoners – both Singaporean and not – embellishing everything with our sambal, from a traditional *nasi lemak* (coconut rice) to an egg and cheese bagel.

**Singaporean cuisine as we know it today has come from a long history of adjusting and adapting, and doing things 'to taste'.**

Many Singaporean dishes are born out of cooks trying to find a taste of home in a foreign land. With different local ingredients, and with different tools, they used their senses to approximate the flavours they missed. Other dishes are born out of entrepreneurial chefs finding their way in a new environment. To make a living, they had to learn to cater to customers from different cultural backgrounds, with different tastes and preferences.

The early Chinese immigrants gave Singapore its national dish, Hainanese chicken rice – but we serve the gently poached chicken with a fiery chilli garlic sauce, instead of the traditional spring onion sauce. Other national classics are born out of a happy collision of cultures. Peranakan cooking combines the fragrant spices and herbs of the Malays with typically Chinese techniques and ingredients – giving us the famous spicy, coconut-laced noodle soup, *nonya laksa*. The incredible array of food you find in Singapore didn't come from simply following iron-clad measurements and methods; it came from decades of changing things up.

**Even today, Singaporean food continues to evolve.**

In Singapore, you can wander down streets lined both with hawker stalls and restaurant chains. As a cosmopolitan city, it's not a surprise to see laksa spaghetti or *ban mian* (handmade noodles) in Thai tom yum broth on menus. Young Singaporean chefs are travelling further abroad and constantly bringing back new ideas. I am writing this with fond memories of a croissant from a young Singaporean bakery on my last visit. The pastry, laminated to buttery perfection, wouldn't have felt out of place in a boulangerie in Paris, but the flaky croissant was filled with black sesame paste and topped with peanut crunch, à la *muah chee* (a local sticky rice flour snack coated with ground sesame seeds or peanuts).

Closer to home, even my mother's signature chicken curry has gone through a number of adaptations over the years. The original recipe came from her Indian brother-in-law, but because it is quite simply not in her blood to follow lists of ingredients and measurements, she has somehow managed to turn it into her own thing. Uncle's use of spices, tomatoes and curry leaves remains, but Mum's version is decidedly less hot and pungent. To suit the tastes of her children, she softens the chilli and spices with a splash more coconut milk, and she also adds lemongrass because they grow rampant in our back garden. It's somewhat like Uncle's, but not quite.

I wrote this book with the intention of not just passing down Singaporean recipes, but sharing a way of cooking, one that's creative, intuitive and fun. It's the way I learnt to cook, and the way I watched my mum cook.

This means you will find tricks, tips and twists to Singaporean hawker favourites. You will find the lesser-seen dishes served only at home among friends and family. You will find new ideas that combine the incredible fresh bounty here with the flavours I've grown up with. You will also find measurements and timings (phew), but I encourage you to keep trying, testing and tasting. As my Auntie would say, one chilli could be spicier than the other…

I hope you see this book as a start to explore Singaporean cooking. As you get more confident, you might find yourself relying more on your senses and experience, and less on my instructions. Feel free to *agak agak* your way through these recipes – I would love it if they became the inspiration for many other signature dishes from your own kitchen.

**HAPPY COOKING X**

# ESSENTIAL SINGAPOREAN VOCABULARY

Besides agak agak, here are a few other words you'll need to know while you cook your way through this book and/or eat your way around Singapore.

**AUNTIE** You'll see Auntie appear in quite a few places in the book. It's not the same person! We use 'Auntie' as a term of endearment for any older woman – so she could easily be my mum's sister, or someone I've just met at the hawker centre.

**HAINANESE** The early Chinese immigrants to Singapore came from different regions of Southern China. The Hainanese are one of them. They arrived in Singapore later and many ended up working as cooks for the British officers or wealthy Peranakans – which explains their huge influence on evolving Singapore's cuisine.

**HOKKIEN** The Hokkiens are also Chinese immigrants to Singapore. Hokkien food is down-to-earth, unfussy in presentation but punchy in flavour. My mum is Hokkien Chinese, so a lot of the home cooking that I grew up with is Hokkien-influenced.

**KOPITIAM** The local term for a casual coffee shop. Here you won't find flat whites, but instead strong coffee (*kopi*) or tea (*teh*) with condensed milk or evaporated milk stirred in.

**KUEH** These refer to bite-sized snacks, both sweet and savoury. They're often made with rice, tapioca or bean starches for a soft or chewy texture. Sweet kueh are often flavoured with coconut and/or pandan.

**MAMAK** This is a term used to describe the Tamil Muslim community and their fiery food, which is often served in unfussy open-air stalls. We lived right by a street with two competing Mamak stalls, so I grew up with plenty of *roti prata* (flaky ghee flatbreads), dipped in curry, for breakfast.

**MEE** The generic Singaporean term for noodles across cultures and languages, be it Malay, Chinese or Indian.

**NASI** Malay for rice.

**NONYA** Nonyas are the women in a Peranakan (see below) household and who, in olden days, ran the kitchen with an iron fist. The two terms are often used interchangeably when used to describe the origins of a dish.

**PERANAKAN** Peranakan people make up a culture born out of the marriage of the local Malays with early immigrant Chinese traders in Singapore. Peranakan/Nonya food combines the local love for spices and herbs, with typically Chinese cooking methods and includes ingredients like pork.

**REMPAH** Essentially a spice paste. Besides spices, fresh aromatic ingredients like shallots, lemongrass and chilli go into a mortar and pestle – or in most modern kitchens, a food processor or blender – to create a rempah. It's also the namesake behind Rempapa Spice Co., the small-batch spice paste business I started in London (rempah.com wasn't available, rempapa.com was).

**SAMBAL** Brought over by our Indonesian neighbours, sambal is the quintessential chilli sauce to dip into or dollop and slather over everything. I share a few variations in the book, but there are endless family recipes.

**TEOCHEW** The Teochews are another Chinese dialect group. Teochew food tends to be lighter and features more pickling, steaming and light braising.

**TZE CHAR** These are hawker stalls serving a huge variety of dishes making for wallet-friendly gatherings with friends and family. *Tze char* chefs love to put creative spins on dishes, so these are often forerunners of new local favourites.

**UNCLE** Similar to 'Auntie', all vaguely middle-aged men are called 'Uncle' in Singapore, whether you are blood related or not, and whether you even know the man or not. I would say 'hello, Uncle' to my friends' fathers and 'thank you, Uncle' to the chicken rice hawker.

**ZHUP** Singlish for sauce. Always ask for extra zhup.

## ESSENTIAL SINGAPOREAN PANTRY

With such diverse multi-cultural influences, it's hard to be a minimalist when putting together a Singaporean pantry. That said, I have tried to narrow down this section to create as simple and essential a list as I can. It's led to many recipe edits and brutal cuts, but you'll find that all the recipes in this book keep to this list.

For storecupboard ingredients, a shop at your nearest Asian supermarket or an online speciality grocer will get you all the essentials you need. These are largely salted or fermented or freeze well, so they will last you for a while. Where possible, I've listed substitutes that can work in a pinch.

For fresh ingredients, I prefer to cook with produce that's largely locally grown and easily obtained from shops or markets here. I do mention a few unusual herbs for you to try, but don't worry if you can't get hold of them, as I've suggested alternatives. Or feel free to play around with what you can find.

## SAUCES AND SEASONINGS

**LIGHT SOY SAUCE** Light soy sauce is salty, versatile and used in all sorts of everyday cooking. Look for a naturally brewed soy sauce for the best flavour. I used Lee Kum Kee while recipe testing for this book. I also like the Japanese brand Kikkoman, but their 'all-purpose soy sauce' tends to be stronger and saltier than Chinese light soy sauce, so hold back and adjust the seasoning as necessary, or go for the lower-salt version.

**DARK SOY SAUCE** Dark soy sauce is made from soy beans that have been fermented for longer. It's darker, less salty and is often sweetened. I use it to add colour and a deeper flavour to braises or marinades.

**KECAP MANIS (SWEET SOY SAUCE)** This soy sauce is rich, dark and glossy, with the consistency of molasses. It tastes sweeter than it is salty and is used to add colour and sweetness to sauces, dips and marinades.

**FISH SAUCE** Made from fermented anchovies, fish sauce is the best way to add a splash of umami to your cooking. Get a premium fish sauce as you will find yourself reaching for it again and again. I am lucky as my Vietnamese sister-in-law brings me bottles from Phu Quoc all the time. Here, I like the brand Red Boat, which is widely available online. For a vegan-friendly substitute, I like Yondu's vegetable umami sauce.

**TAUCHEO** Like soy sauce, taucheo is made from fermented salted soy beans, but the soy beans are left whole. We use it mashed up in sauces or stir-fries. Yeo's is the most common brand here, found in Asian stores or online. If you really can't get hold of it, Japanese white miso paste will work in a pinch for the recipes in this book.

**SHRIMP PASTE** Made from fermented shrimps, shrimp paste can be quite pungent when raw, but it mellows and becomes deep, aromatic and savoury once cooked. In Singapore, we use the kind that comes in a solid block called *belacan*, or *terasi* in Indonesia. Break off as needed for the recipe and make sure you haven't picked the same day to hang your laundry in the kitchen! If you can't find belacan, you can substitute this with readily available jarred Thai shrimp paste.

**OYSTER SAUCE** This sauce is made of oyster extract and tastes savoury, sweet and salty all at once. There are plenty of recipes in this book that can be turned vegan-friendly just by replacing the oyster sauce with a plant-based version. Lee Kum Kee makes a great one using mushrooms instead of oyster, which is labelled as 'vegetarian stir-fry sauce'.

**SHAOXING RICE WINE** This is a shelf-stable cooking rice wine, so it's handy to have a bottle in your pantry. We add a splash to Chinese-influenced stir-fries, braises and marinades for its heady aroma. If you can't get hold of it, use a medium-dry sherry.

**SESAME OIL** We use sesame oil to add a wonderful nutty aroma to all sorts of dishes, especially those with Chinese origins. Look for pure toasted sesame oil, not blended oils.

## SPICES AND CHILLIES

**BIRD'S EYE CHILLIES** Sometimes called Thai chillies in the supermarkets. These chillies are tiny but pack a punch, which is why in Singapore we would call someone who's petite but bold a *chilli padi* (its Malay name). A hot tip: stick them whole in the freezer. They freeze beautifully and thaw in seconds under warm running tap water.

**FRESH LARGE CHILLIES** You'll also see me calling for these chillies, green or red, in garnishes or spice pastes. They're bigger and less spicy, so are perfect for when you need large quantities for their flavour and colour but don't want to set your mouth on fire. They can vary in variety (and hence heat) in the shops, so take a cautious nibble first and adjust the recipe quantities as needed.

**DRIED CHILLIES AND CHILLI POWDER** We use dried chillies, whole or ground, for their deeper colour and flavour. Again, these can vary in variety and heat. For consistency, I've used mild red Kashmiri dried chillies and chilli powder while recipe testing.

**GROUND SPICES** Use them and replace them regularly, as the forgotten jar at the back of your shelf is likely to taste of nothing more than dust. The ground spices we most commonly use are turmeric, cumin, coriander, white pepper and five-spice.

**WHOLE SPICES** These are spices that we often use in whole form, left to simmer for hours in a braise or to sizzle in hot oil. Our favourites are cinnamon bark, star anise, cardamom pods, cumin seeds, cloves, white peppercorns and mustard seeds.

## HERBS AND AROMATICS

**FRAGRANT LEAFY HERBS**
These are the herbs you'll find stirred into or sprinkled over dishes in this book: coriander (cilantro), spring onions (scallions), mint, Thai basil, laksa leaf.

Most are readily available, save for laksa leaf. Also known as hot mint or Vietnamese coriander, its citrusy, peppery flavour is definitive in laksa, hence its Singaporean name. You can find laksa leaves at Asian stores, or sometimes at the herb stall at farmers' markets. If you can't get hold of it, use a mix of fresh mint and coriander leaves.

**ROOTS AND BULBS** These are the aromatic ingredients most often used as the base for spice pastes or at the start of cooking: shallots, garlic, ginger and galangal. You probably have most of these at home, except for the galangal. It looks very similar to ginger but tastes quite different; it's sharp and piney rather than earthy and spicy, so they cannot be substituted for each other. You can find fresh galangal at any Asian store. Otherwise, jarred galangal paste works ok for the recipes in this book and can be found at most large supermarkets.

**LEMONGRASS** I love that you can find fresh lemongrass in the herb aisles of most supermarkets nowadays. It adds an earthy, lemony flavour to everything from a curry to a marinade. Remove any woody outer layers and tops of the lemongrass before slicing and adding to a spice paste; or bash to release its citrus oils and throw it whole into a simmering pot.

**LIME LEAVES** These perfumed leaves come from the makrut lime tree. They can be crushed and simmered whole, or used as a finishing herb by cutting off the stem in the middle and slicing the tender leaf very thinly. You can find them fresh at most big supermarkets now, but in a pinch, freshly grated lime zest will do the trick.

**CURRY LEAVES** These shiny green leaves smell of pepper and orange peel. Once released into hot oil, they crackle and infuse the oil with their divine flavour. They are often used in – you guessed it – curries. But the inventive cooks of Singapore also love adding curry leaves to all sorts of new creative dishes, such as Cereal Prawns (page 112). Sprigs of fresh leaves can be bought easily online, from Indian grocers or occasionally in big supermarkets. Dried leaves lack the same intensity, but if you must use them, double the amount used.

**PANDAN** These leaves have a sweet, grassy fragrance and are used in both sweet and savoury cooking. Knot the leaves to bruise them and release their flavour. Or blitz with water/coconut milk to extract their gorgeous green juices, and use them to naturally dye and flavour puddings. You can find pandan leaves fresh or frozen in Asian stores. I also keep Koepoe Pandan Paste, which is widely available online, as a handy storecupboard flavouring. In fact, I recommend it over fresh in certain recipes, like the Pandan Swiss Roll (page 184).

# TINS AND PACKETS

**COCONUT MILK** I look straight at the ingredients list when I'm buying coconut milk. A good coconut milk should have more than 50 per cent coconut extract, and the rest of the tin should be made up of just water. Guar gum is sometimes added to cheat a creamy texture, especially when the coconut content is low, but instead it gives coconut milk an odd gluey texture.

**TAMARIND** I love using tamarind to add a sweet and sour zing to dishes. It comes in many forms: fresh in pods, as a pulp in cellophane-wrapped blocks, or as a concentrated purée in plastic or glass jars. For ease and consistency, I use tamarind paste or concentrate. Make sure to get one that's smooth and a medium brown – most Thai, Vietnamese or supermarket own-brands will be perfect. Tamarind pastes from Indian brands are black and sticky and too intensely sharp for the recipes in this book.

**GULA MELAKA (COCONUT PALM SUGAR)** This unrefined dark palm sugar is made from the sap of coconut palms. Unlike caster (superfine) sugar, it doesn't just taste sweet, it has a rich, caramel-like colour and flavour that's heavenly in sweet treats. *Gula melaka* traditionally comes in solid cylindrical blocks, so you have to grate it or melt it into a syrup to use it. You can also find it as soft crystals on supermarket shelves, packaged as 'coconut palm sugar' or 'coconut sugar'.

**DRIED SHRIMPS** These tiny shrimps are packed with the sweet-salty flavour of the sea. Soak in warm water to soften before chopping up and adding to stir-fries or spice pastes. I will always call for you to save that soaking liquid – it's pretty much a quick shrimp-flavoured stock and can be used to add flavour to dishes. It's useful to get a small packet of dried shrimps on your trip to the Asian supermarket, as they keep for months in your fridge.

**DRIED SHIITAKE MUSHROOMS** Whilst you can find fresh shiitake mushrooms at almost any supermarket these days, it's also worth getting a bag of the dried mushrooms, as these have a more concentrated flavour and meaty texture. Let them plump up in braising sauces, or soak them before use in warm water until they soften. Similarly, always save the soaking liquid to use as a mushroom stock.

# RICE TO EVERY

**CHAPTER ONE**

# GO WITH THING

## CHAPTER ONE

# ONE

Growing up, rice was always the reassuring constant on the dinner table. Everyone would be sitting in front of a plate or bowl of steaming hot rice, and the centre of the table would be filled with deep sharing platters of food for everyone to help themselves, spooning delicious things onto their rice. Occasionally, my dad would ask if anyone needed a rice top-up, and hands would go up. It's a happy, noisy, social way to eat and it's still the way I like to eat with my friends and family.

The default rice we would eat with a meal like this was plain steamed long-grain rice – no salt, no oil. I use jasmine when I want a fluffy, chewy bite and basmati when I want looser-flowing grains. On special occasions, I would stir in coconut milk or herbs for extra fragrance, or turmeric to dye it a glorious golden colour. The rice recipes in this section are all basic and unadorned, so you can mix and match them with other dishes from the next few sections – curries, broths, braises, feasting food, stir-fries and simple sides – to make a complete meal.

### NOTE

Because rice is such a staple of Singaporean food, you will find it cooked in myriad other ways – fried with *sambal* for a feisty *nasi goreng* or simmered in stock until the grains turn to porridge. These more substantial rice dishes are mostly eaten on their own, without sides – flick to Chapter 6 (One-Dish Meals) on page 128 for those recipes.

# Everyday Rice

Once you master the basics of rice, you'll never go back to a microwaveable pack. It really isn't difficult; and it smells and tastes infinitely better. This is the method I use for preparing and cooking all sorts of long-grain rice, including jasmine and basmati.

### Rinse, rinse, rinse

Rinsing rice removes any surface starch, preventing clumpy cooked rice. Place the uncooked grains in the pot with plenty of water, then swirl and swish using your hands. Pour away the cloudy water, then do it twice more or until the water runs relatively clear. If using basmati, and if you have the time, soak the rice for 15–30 minutes before that last rinse, as this gives you longer, looser grains.

### Now add just the right amount of fresh water

I was taught to place my palm flat just above the grains until the water covers my knuckles. If you must have a measurement, to feed two, you will need about 150 g (5½ oz/¾ cup) uncooked rice and 250 ml (8 fl oz/1 cup) water.

You will notice in both cooking methods opposite that there's no water to tip away at the end. The rice steams and absorbs all the water by the end of the cooking time. You never want to boil rice like you would pasta. I shudder to think of all that goodness going down the drain.

### Let the rice cooker do its magic

Most Asians own a rice cooker. It's a worthy investment, especially if you eat rice almost every day. If you don't, I guarantee a rice cooker will turn you into a regular rice-eater. For the converted, the only step left at this stage is to press the 'cook' button. When the rice is cooked, leave it in the 'keep warm' stage for another 5 minutes before opening the lid. Inhale its wonderful fragrance and give it a fluff with a rice paddle or rubber spatula (a fork will break up the grains). Serve immediately, or pop the lid back on and have the rice stay warm until you're ready to serve.

### If you must hover over a saucepan …

Bring the rice and water to a boil over medium–high heat. Give the rice a stir to loosen the grains sticking to the bottom. Simmer, uncovered, until most of the water has been absorbed. You will see little craters in the rice. Cover with a tight-fitting lid and turn the heat down as low as you can for 15 minutes. Turn the heat off and let the rice sit, still covered, for another 10 minutes so it finishes steaming in the residual heat of the pot.

If you're scaling up, make sure to scale up your saucepan as well! For example, I would use a 15-cm (6-in) saucepan for rice for two; 20-cm (8-in) saucepan for rice for four to six. Using a tiny saucepan to cook a large quantity of rice will lead to undercooked rice at the top and gummy rice at the bottom.

SERVES 3–4 AS A SIDE

# Pandan Jasmine Rice

Once you've got the basics down, it's only a matter of adding different herbs, spices and/or seasonings for flavoured rice. Pandan rice is one of my favourites – the sweet, grassy smell of pandan leaves only elevates the natural fragrance of jasmine rice. This goes well with everything, especially curries.

300 g (10½ oz/1½ cups) white jasmine rice
2–3 pandan leaves
1 tbsp coconut oil, or 3 tbsp coconut milk
1 tsp fine sea salt
about 500 ml (17 fl oz/2 cups) water

Rinse the rice twice in a sieve (fine mesh strainer) under cold running water and set aside in a rice cooker or saucepan.

You have two options with the pandan leaves.

Option one is to simply tie the leaves into knots and toss them on top of the rice as it cooks. Then combine the rice with the coconut oil or milk, salt and the water – just up to your knuckles with your palm flat over the grains.

Option two is to cut the leaves into small pieces, blend them in a mini blender with a splash of water, then strain, discarding the solids but keeping the bright green pandan juice to cook the rice with. The latter method infuses the rice with a stronger fragrance and dyes it a beautiful pale green as it cooks. Top up the pandan juice with enough water to make 500 ml (18 fl oz/2 cups). Add the pandan juice to the rice (again, just up to your knuckles with your palm flat over the grains), along with the coconut oil or milk and salt.

With either option, cook in the rice cooker or on the stovetop following the instructions on page 30, before fluffing up with a fork and serving.

SERVES 3–4 AS A SIDE

# Coconut Rice

*Nasi lemak* is one of the definitive rice dishes of the Malay community in Singapore. Most Singaporeans will think of *nasi lemak* not simply as coconut rice, but as rice with all its trimmings: crispy salty fried anchovies, roasted peanuts and sweet *sambal tumis* (page 204). Nonetheless this indulgent rice is a wonderful accompaniment to all sorts of dishes – particularly the spicy ones in this book. I make my *nasi lemak* with basmati rice, as the light, fluffy grains balance the richness of the coconut milk better. An easy way to remember the ratios for this recipe is to replace roughly half the water with coconut milk.

300 g (10½ oz/1½ cups) white basmati rice
1 lemongrass stalk, or 1 pandan leaf (optional)
250 ml (8 fl oz/1 cup) coconut milk
1 tsp fine sea salt
about 250 ml (8 fl oz/1 cup) water

Rinse the rice in a sieve (fine mesh strainer) under cold running water, then leave to soak in a bowl of cold water for 15–30 minutes. Drain.

If using the herbs, bash the lemongrass or knot the pandan leaf to bruise it and help it release its flavour better.

Combine the drained rice with the herbs, if using, coconut milk and salt and top up with the water – just up to your knuckles with your palm flat over the grains. Cook in a rice cooker or on the stovetop following the instructions on page 30, before fluffing up with a fork and serving.

RICE TO GO WITH EVERYTHING

# Fresh Herb Rice Salad

*Nasi ulam* is a refreshing accompaniment and one I like to roll out for summer to serve alongside barbecued dishes. There are many variations of this rice salad, but they all involve a good amount and variety of fresh herbs stirred into cooled rice. The traditional list of ingredients includes salted dried fish and wild herbs like ginger torch flowers. In my version I've left out any impossible-to-find herbs and used toasted coconut for fragrance.

50 g (1¾ oz/⅔ cup) desiccated (shredded) coconut
2 shallots, finely chopped
thumb-sized piece (15 g/½ oz) fresh ginger, peeled and finely chopped
6 lime leaves, stalks removed and finely sliced
handful (100 g/3½ oz) of mint leaves, finely sliced
handful (100 g/3½ oz) of coriander (cilantro) leaves and stalks, finely sliced
handful (100 g/3½ oz) of Thai basil leaves, finely sliced
500 g (1 lb 2 oz/2¾ cups) cooked basmati rice, cooled
1 tsp fine sea salt, or to taste
1 tsp freshly ground white pepper
juice and zest of 1 lime (about 2 tbsp juice)

In a frying pan over medium heat, toast the coconut, stirring occasionally to make sure it colours evenly and does not burn. Once light golden, set aside off the heat – it will continue to darken as it cools.

In a big bowl, combine all the ingredients and mix well. Check for seasoning, adjusting as needed.

SERVES 3–4 AS A SIDE

# Plain Congee

Growing up in Singapore, I knew congee in its many guises and by its many names. *Zhou* (Mandarin), *ber* (Hokkien), *jook* (Cantonese), *mui* (Teochew) or *bubur* (Malay) – whatever it's called, it is what I instantly reach for when I come back from an indulgent holiday or when I'm feeling sniffly and sorry for myself. Essentially, it is simply rice cooked in stock or water until the grains have all disintegrated into a porridge. You can cook it from scratch, or use leftover rice to halve the cooking time. This is a recipe for the most unadorned form of congee; not even salt is added, as we often have this soothing, soft porridge with salty braises, stir-fries and pickles.

300 g (10½ oz/1½ cups) cooked jasmine rice
1 litre (34 fl oz/4½ cups) water or homemade stock (broth) (page 67)

Bring the cooked rice and water or stock to the boil in a saucepan over high heat. Cover, turn the heat down to low, then simmer for 20–30 minutes. Stir occasionally to loosen any grains that are sticking to the bottom and top up with more water as necessary. It's ready when the rice grains are plump and have started to disintegrate.

NOTE

We often turn this into a more substantial one-dish meal by adding seasoned chicken or vegetable stock (broth), simmering with vegetables or minced (ground) pork, or poaching an egg or thinly sliced fish in the congee at the last minute. Get creative! See Hot Smoked Mackerel and Ginger Congee, page 156, for an example.

SERVES 3–4 AS A SIDE

# Steamed Fragrant Sticky Rice

Sticky, or glutinous, rice is, as its name suggests, sticky and wonderfully chewy when steamed. However, it does not, as its name might suggest, contain gluten. We tend to save sticky rice for special occasions as it requires a bit more thought – the grains must be soaked ahead, then cooked in a steamer rather than the trusty old rice cooker. Unlike the Thais, we rarely serve plain sticky rice. It will be infused with flavour from Chinese sausage and/or dried shiitake mushrooms or, more simply, infused with heavenly fragrance from fried shallots. I love this with all sorts of braises or steamed dishes, or sometimes simply on its own for breakfast.

400 g (14 oz/2 cups) glutinous rice
2 big pinches (about ½ tsp) of fine sea salt
2 tbsp Fried Shallot Oil (page 209)
2 tbsp Fried Shallots (page 209)

Rinse the glutinous rice in a sieve (fine mesh strainer) under cold running water, then transfer to a bowl and cover with plenty of cold water, stir in the salt and leave to soak overnight.

The next day, drain the rice and mix well with the shallot oil. Transfer to a shallow plate that will fit into your steamer and scatter the fried shallots over the rice.

Cover and steam for 20 minutes. Stir the rice to bring any grains at the bottom to the top, then continue steaming for another 5–10 minutes.

At the end of the steaming time, turn off the heat and leave the rice in the steamer for another 5 minutes or until you are ready to serve. Keep it covered, as the rice will dry out if it is exposed to the air as it cools.

RICE TO GO WITH EVERYTHING

SERVES 3–4 AS A SIDE

# Yellow Sticky Rice

This is glutinous rice that's cooked with coconut milk and dyed golden with ground turmeric. *Nasi kunyit* is most often served during Malay or Peranakan celebratory feasts. Here, I like to pull it out of the bag for dinner parties or supper clubs, as it not only tastes great but looks glorious too.

400 g (14 oz/2 cups) glutinous rice
1 tbsp ground turmeric
2 big pinches (about ½ tsp) of fine sea salt
2 pandan leaves (optional)
100 ml (3½ fl oz/scant ½ cup) coconut milk
juice of ½ lime

Rinse the glutinous rice in a sieve (fine mesh strainer) under cold running water, then transfer to a bowl and cover with plenty of cold water and stir in the turmeric and salt. Leave to soak overnight.

The next day, drain the rice and transfer to a shallow plate that will fit into your steamer. Tie the pandan leaves, if using, into knots and place on top of the rice.

Cover and steam for 20 minutes. Drizzle the coconut milk over the rice, then replace the lid and continue steaming for another 10 minutes.

At the end of the steaming time, turn off the heat and leave the rice in the steamer for another 5 minutes. When you're ready to serve, finish by squeezing the lime juice over.

While glutinous rice is the traditional grain used here, long-grain rice is a worthy alternative and one that I often favour at home. Follow the recipe for Coconut Rice (page 33) and stir in a heaped teaspoon of ground turmeric to turn it golden.

# CUR

## CHAPTER TWO

CHAPTER TWO

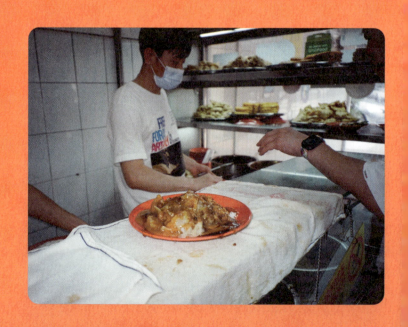

## TWO

Nothing shows off Singapore's diversity quite like our love for curry. Because of Singapore's proximity to the Indonesian Spice Islands, its immigrant Indian population and its historical role as a port city, every culture has learnt to use and embrace different spices in their cooking.

In fact, my fondest memory of curry is something that no one outside of Singapore would recognise. My dad ran a hardware shop in Jalan Besar and we would often head to the famous Hainanese curry rice stall nearby. There, plates of rice would be piled with scissors-cut fried pork chop and *chap chye* (braised cabbage), then drenched in a dark soy braising sauce *AND* a sweet, mildly spiced curry. It was an assault on the senses – the perfect first introduction to curry for a five-year-old.

I soon graduated to spicier things. There were the Mamak curries – hot lentil dals made for dunking flaky *roti prata* (ghee flatbreads) into. There were the South Indian curries – fish heads simmered with tamarind, and mutton with potatoes. There were the Malay curries – slow-cooked rendang, and vegetable stews that were sweet and rich with coconut. There were the Nonya curries, too – fragrant and layered with pungent nuts and spices as well as decidedly Chinese ingredients like pork belly.

In this chapter, I've tried to include recipes that give you a spread of flavours across this spectacular world of curries, but these are really only the tip of the iceberg.

### NOTE

You will notice that many of the recipes in this section start with a *rempah* (spice paste). A kickass *rempah* is the base for a kickass curry, but I would encourage you to use this aromatic blend in other parts of your cooking, too. All spice pastes freeze beautifully and can be made ahead in bigger batches. In fact, when we first launched Rempapa Spice Co., we sold the spice pastes in little frozen packets at the farmers' market. We would stress to customers that they could do more than just stir in coconut milk. Use any of the curry pastes here to marinate meats before a barbecue or to add kick to a stir-fry (see Uncle's 'Dry' Laksa on page 138).

SERVES 3–4

# Chicken in Red Sauce

The red sauce here is a cut above Heinz! The deep red colour in *ayam masak merah* comes from tomatoes, dried red chillies and, yes, there is a little squirt of ketchup. The chicken is marinated first in turmeric, then fried, before being simmered for an hour with spices and tomatoes. It's the slow cooking of the tomatoes and chilli in oil that concentrates and transforms them into a jammy sweetness, much like sun-dried tomatoes. I like to use fresh tomatoes, especially in summer when they are just bursting with sweetness, but in winter, feel free to substitute these for the same quantity of tinned chopped tomatoes.

750 g (1 lb 10 oz) chicken thighs, skin on and bone in
½ tsp ground turmeric
2 big pinches of coarse sea salt
3–4 tbsp vegetable oil
4 cardamom pods, lightly bashed
4 cloves
4 tbsp tomato ketchup
2 medium (100 g/3½ oz) ripe tomatoes, roughly chopped
about 250 ml (8 fl oz/1 cup) water
1 tsp fine sea salt, or to taste
1½ tsp light brown sugar, or to taste
juice of ½ lime
handful of coriander (cilantro), to serve
1 red chilli, thinly sliced, to serve

### FOR THE REMPAH (SPICE PASTE)

1 red onion, roughly chopped
2 lemongrass stalks, base only, finely chopped
thumb-sized piece (15 g/½ oz) of fresh ginger, peeled and roughly chopped
2 garlic cloves
10 dried red Kashmiri chillies, soaked in hot water until soft

Pound all the spice paste ingredients using a pestle and mortar or whizz in a small blender until you get a fine paste. Rub the chicken with the turmeric and coarse sea salt.

Add enough oil to just cover the base of a shallow casserole pot (Dutch oven) set over medium heat. Once the oil is hot, add the chicken thighs skin-side down. Leave them to fry over medium–low heat until golden – don't be nosy and keep poking at them! Once golden, flip and fry until golden on the other side. Remove and set aside on kitchen paper (paper towels).

In the remaining oil in the pot, fry the whole spices, followed by the spice paste for 15 minutes, or until the oil separates from the paste.

Now stir in the ketchup and chopped tomatoes and cook until the tomatoes have softened. Return the chicken to the pot along with the water, salt and sugar.

Bring the whole pot to a gentle boil, then lower the heat and let simmer, partially covered, for about 1 hour. The curry is ready when the chicken is tender and the sauce is a rich, paste-like consistency. If it's still too wet, uncover and cook to reduce the sauce.

Finish with a squeeze of lime, then taste again for seasoning. Once you're happy, sprinkle with coriander and chilli to serve.

SERVES 3–4

# Lime Leaf Chicken Curry

I have a huge recipe bank of chicken curries, but this is one I make time and time again. No dried spices are used, just lots of fresh chilli, herbs and aromatics – the star of which is the lime leaf. As the curry bubbles away, these scented leaves infuse the chicken with a wonderful perfumed fragrance. I also add lime juice and zest at the very last minute for an extra citrusy lift.

2 tbsp vegetable oil
750 g (1 lb 10 oz) chicken thighs or drumsticks, skin on and bone in
200 ml (7 fl oz/generous ¾ cup) coconut milk
6 lime leaves, left whole and crushed lightly
about 250 ml (8 fl oz/1 cup) water
1 tsp fine sea salt, or to taste
¾ tsp sugar, or to taste
zest of 1 lime, juice of ½ (1 tbsp)

FOR THE REMPAH (SPICE PASTE)

thumb-sized piece (15 g/½ oz) galangal, roughly chopped, or 1 tbsp galangal paste
2 lemongrass stalks, base only, finely chopped
3 garlic cloves
200 g (7 oz) shallots, roughly chopped
2 large fresh red chillies, roughly chopped

Pound all the spice paste ingredients using a pestle and mortar or whizz in a small blender until you get a fine paste.

In a shallow casserole pot (Dutch oven), fry the spice paste in the oil over medium–low heat, stirring often, for 20 minutes or until the oil separates from the paste. Add the chicken and coat with the spice paste.

Next, turn up the heat and stir in the coconut milk and lime leaves. Add just enough water to cover the chicken, then season with the salt and sugar.

Bring the whole pot to a gentle boil, then lower the heat to a simmer. Cook, partially covered, for 1 hour, then uncover and simmer for another 5 minutes, spooning the sauce over the chicken as it thickens.

Finish with the lime zest and juice. Taste again for seasoning, adjusting with more salt or sugar, if you like.

SERVES 3–4

# Hainanese Pork and New Potato Curry

This recipe is kudos to my earliest taste and memory of curry. Hainanese curry is sweet and mild, but while it's gentle on the sinuses, it packs a punch with fragrant spices, lemongrass and soy sauce. I love adding potatoes to curry as they soak up all the flavour from the sauce while cooking. Don't use floury potatoes as they will fall apart in the sauce; I tend to go for baby new potatoes as they have the perfect texture, and their small sizes and thin skins mean you don't have to bother with peeling or chopping.

500 g (1 lb 2 oz) pork shoulder, cut into 3 cm (1¼ in) chunks
1 cinnamon stick
2 star anise
2 lemongrass stalks, bashed lightly
4 tbsp vegetable oil
200 ml (7 fl oz/generous ¾ cup) coconut milk
about 250 ml (8 fl oz/1 cup) water
250 g (9 oz) baby new potatoes, left whole, larger ones halved
3 tbsp light soy sauce, or to taste
2 tsp light brown sugar, or to taste

FOR THE REMPAH (SPICE PASTE)

100 g (3½ oz) shallots, roughly chopped
thumb-sized piece (15 g/½ oz) fresh ginger, peeled and roughly chopped
4 garlic cloves, peeled
2 tsp Kashmiri chilli powder
1 tsp ground white pepper
1 tsp ground coriander
1 tsp ground turmeric
½ tsp ground cumin
big pinch of fine sea salt

For the spice paste, pound the shallots, ginger and garlic using a pestle and mortar or whizz in a small blender until you get a fine paste, before mixing in the ground spices and salt. Coat the pork chunks with the spice paste and set aside to marinate for 15 minutes.

In a wok or shallow casserole pot (Dutch oven), fry the whole spices and lemongrass in the oil over medium heat for about 1 minute, to help release their fragrance.

Add the marinated pork, scraping in all the spice paste, then fry for about 10 minutes, or until the pork browns.

Next, stir in the coconut milk and enough of the water to just cover the pork. Bring to a gentle boil, then turn the heat down to low and cook, partially covered, for 1 hours 30 minutes.

Gently tip in the potatoes and season the curry with soy sauce and sugar. Pop the lid back on and cook for another 20 minutes, or until the pork and potatoes are very tender. Taste and adjust seasoning with more soy sauce or sugar, if you like.

SERVES 4–6

# 8-hour Ox Cheek Rendang

A rendang is a 'dry' curry. You might be tempted to stop the process too soon – not least because it smells incredibly delicious even halfway through – but be patient! The hours of simmering turn the cooking process from boiling to frying; as the liquid evaporates, the meat ends up caramelising in its own fat and the fat that separates from the coconut milk. This gives the rendang its glorious deep colour and intense, rich flavours.

4 tbsp vegetable oil
800 g (1 lb 12 oz) ox cheek, trimmed and cut into 3 cm (1¼ in) chunks
2 pinches of coarse sea salt
1 cinnamon bark
4 star anise
4 cloves
6 cardamom pods, crushed
2 lemongrass stalks, bashed
400 ml (14 fl oz/generous 1½ cups) coconut milk
4 tbsp tamarind paste
8 lime leaves, stalks removed and finely sliced
2 tsp fine sea salt, or to taste
4 tbsp light brown sugar
about 500 ml (17 fl oz/2 cups) water
4 tbsp desiccated (shredded) coconut
handful of fresh coriander (cilantro), chopped, to serve

FOR THE REMPAH (SPICE PASTE)

200 g (7 oz) shallots, roughly chopped
1 garlic bulb, cloves separated
4 lemongrass stalks, base only, finely chopped
1 thumb-sized piece (15 g/½ oz) fresh galangal, roughly chopped, or 1 tbsp galangal paste
1 thumb-sized piece (15 g/½ oz) fresh ginger, roughly chopped
10 dried red chillies, soaked in hot water until soft

Pound all the spice paste ingredients using a pestle and mortar or whizz in a small blender until you get a fine paste.

In a deep ovenproof casserole pot (Dutch oven), heat the oil over medium heat. Sprinkle the ox cheek with salt, then sear in the hot pot until browned. Remove and set aside.

To the remaining oil in the pot, add the whole spices and lemongrass stalks, followed by the rempah. Fry until aromatic, about 10 minutes.

Preheat the oven to 170°C/150°C fan/350°F/gas mark 3.

Stir the coconut milk and tamarind into the spices, scraping the bottom of the pot to loosen any browned bits. Return the ox cheek to the pot, along with the lime leaves, salt, sugar and just enough of the water to cover the meat.

Bring to a gentle boil, then cover and place the whole pot in the oven for 7 hours. Midway through, toast the coconut in a dry pan until golden and add to the rendang. Stir through to make sure the ingredients aren't catching at the bottom of the pot.

The rendang is ready when the meat is fall-apart tender and the sauce is rich and thick – just coating the meat. Taste for seasoning, adding more salt or sugar if you like, and serve scattered with coriander.

Because of the time commitment involved, I never make rendang in a batch smaller than this. Leftovers (if any!) freeze beautifully for rainy days.

SERVES 3–4

# Assam Fish, Runner Bean and Tomato Curry

Fish-head curry is one of Singapore's most famous dishes. First invented by an innovative Keralan chef, it brings together South Indian spices and the Chinese love for steamed fish head. Its popularity has spawned countless versions of this delicacy, with Chinese, Malay and Nonya chefs serving up their own take on fish-head curry. My favourite version uses tamarind *(assam)* as a base, making for a hot, tangy curry. While I did enjoy watching my visiting British friends' fearful faces as they took their first bites (and loved it), I've learnt to adapt the dish for simpler, everyday cooking in London, using easier-to-find ingredients. Instead of a massive fish head and okra, I like using hake, runner beans and tomato. Any firm white fish will do, the key is to poach the fish very gently in the tamarind sauce so it stays delicate and flaky.

400 g (14 oz) hake or any firm white fish fillets
big pinch of coarse sea salt
3 tbsp vegetable oil
1 tsp black mustard seeds
10 fresh curry leaves
3 tbsp tamarind paste
100 ml (3½ fl oz/scant 1½ cup) coconut milk
400 ml (14 fl oz/generous 1½ cups) water
2 tsp fine sea salt, or to taste
1 tbsp light brown sugar, or to taste
2 medium tomatoes, cut into quarters
200 g (7 oz) runner beans, stringed and sliced diagonally
handful of fresh coriander (cilantro), roughly chopped

FOR THE REMPAH (SPICE PASTE)

1 small onion, roughly chopped
4 garlic cloves
thumb-sized piece (15 g/½ oz) fresh ginger, peeled and roughly chopped
1 tbsp Kashmiri chilli powder
½ tsp ground turmeric
½ tsp ground cumin
½ tsp ground coriander

Sprinkle the fish with the sea salt and set aside.

Pound all the spice paste ingredients using a pestle and mortar or whizz in a small blender until you get a fine paste. If using a blender, you might find you need to add 1–2 tablespoons of water.

Make sure you've got a shallow pot or pan that's wide enough to fit your fish in a single layer. Heat the oil in the pot over medium heat, then add the mustard seeds and curry leaves. Once the mustard seeds start to pop, add the spice paste and fry, stirring often, until the oil separates from the paste, about 15 minutes.

Stir in the tamarind paste, coconut milk, water, salt and sugar to taste. Bring everything to a gentle boil, then add the tomatoes and runner beans. Simmer, with the lid off, until the tomatoes soften and the runner beans are tender.

Now add the fish fillets, making sure they're mostly submerged in the curry sauce. Cover, turn the heat to low and let the fish poach in the curry for 3–5 minutes, until opaque and just cooked through.

Taste and adjust seasoning with a pinch more salt or sugar, if you like, before serving sprinkled with fresh coriander.

SERVES 3–4

# Peranakan Prawn and Pineapple Curry

While I love pineapple fresh and tossed in a salad, I have a real fondness for cooked pineapple. A flash on a hot grill, or a brief simmer in the pan transforms the fruit – heat tenderises it and concentrates its flavour. In this classic Peranakan curry, golden chunks of pineapple are paired with fresh king prawns (shrimp). Both ingredients have a natural sweetness that complement each other beautifully – the prawns are sweet and savoury while the pineapples are sweet and sour. I like to sprinkle over thinly shredded lime leaves right at the end. This is a garnish used in many sweet coconut-based curries, because the perfumed leaves don't only look pretty, they give the dish a bright, citrusy lift.

3–4 tbsp vegetable oil
200 ml (7 fl oz/generous ¾ cup) coconut milk
about 200 ml (7 fl oz/generous ¾ cup) water
1 tsp sea salt, or to taste
1 tsp light brown sugar, or to taste
350 g (12 oz) raw jumbo king prawns (shrimp), peeled, tails on
200 g (7 oz) pineapple, peeled and cut in triangles
2 lime leaves, stalks removed and finely sliced

FOR THE REMPAH (SPICE PASTE)

1 small onion, roughly chopped
thumb-sized piece (15 g/½ oz) fresh ginger, peeled and roughly chopped
2 lemongrass stalks, base only, finely chopped
1 large fresh red chilli, roughly chopped
½ tsp ground turmeric
¼ tsp ground coriander

Pound all the spice paste ingredients using a pestle and mortar or whizz in a small blender until you get a fine paste.

Add the oil to a shallow pot or large frying pan set over medium heat. Once the oil is hot, fry the spice paste for about 10 minutes until very fragrant. Turn the heat up, stir in the coconut milk, water, salt and sugar.

Once bubbling, add the prawns to the pan, along with the pineapple pieces. Cover, turn the heat down to low and simmer for 3–4 minutes until the prawns turn orange and are just cooked.

To finish, taste and season with more salt or sugar, if you like, then sprinkle over the shredded lime leaves.

SERVES 3–4

# Vegetables and Tofu Puffs in Coconut Milk

On the surface, *sayur lodeh* might look like any vegetable curry, but it is much more than that. In fact, for those expecting the full, pungent force of a classic Indian or Thai curry, you might be surprised to find that this dish is not heavily spiced at all. I like to think of it instead as a vegetable stew, laced with coconut and fragrant lemongrass. All the ingredients come together, very thoughtfully, to create something more than the sum of its parts – and something that's utterly delicious. The cabbage and carrots add sweetness, the dried shrimp add savouriness, the green beans give colour and bite, the lemongrass adds fragrance and the tofu puffs soak up the delicious coconut broth like little sponges.

2 tbsp vegetable oil
200 ml (7 fl oz/generous ¾ cup) coconut milk
500 ml (17 fl oz/2 cups) water
1½ tsp fine sea salt, or to taste
1½ tsp light brown sugar, or to taste
2 large carrots, sliced into 1 cm (½ in) rounds
½ pointed (sweetheart) cabbage, chopped into 3 cm (1¼ in) large pieces
70 g (2½ oz) tofu puffs, halved diagonally into triangles
100 g (2½ oz) green beans, halved into finger-length pieces

FOR THE REMPAH (SPICE PASTE)

3 tbsp dried shrimps (see Note)
100 g (3½ oz) shallots, roughly chopped
1 large (25 g/1 oz) red chilli, roughly chopped
4 garlic cloves
1 tbsp ground turmeric
2 lemongrass stalks, base only, finely chopped

First make the spice paste. Soak the dried shrimp in a bowl of just enough hot water to cover until softened, about 5 minutes. Drain, reserving the soaking liquid for later, and pound all the spice paste ingredients using a pestle and mortar or whizz in a small blender until you get a fine paste.

In a large pot, fry the rempah in the oil over medium heat, stirring to prevent it burning. Cook until very fragrant, about 10 minutes.

Add the coconut milk, water and reserved shrimp soaking liquid. Season with the salt and sugar. Bring everything to a gentle boil, before adding the carrots and cabbage.

Cover, turn the heat down to low and simmer until the vegetables are tender, but not mushy. Tip in the tofu puffs and green beans and let it bubble away for another few minutes, uncovered, until the beans are cooked but still bright green.

The vegetables lend natural sweetness to the coconut broth, while the dried shrimps add saltiness, so taste and check for seasoning again at the end, adding more salt and sugar as needed.

An authentic *sayur lodeh* has dried shrimp in it, but for a vegan-friendly version, simply skip this ingredient and season with a touch more salt.

SERVES 3–4

# Roast Pumpkin Masak Lemak

*'Masak lemak'* simply means 'to cook in coconut milk'. This is a recipe that can work with all sorts of ingredients. Its versatility means I often serve a variation of this when I have non-meat-eating guests over – fresh greens in spring, aubergines (eggplants) in summer, pumpkin or squash in autumn and cavolo nero in winter.

1 kg (2 lb 4 oz) pumpkin or sweet winter squash (I used red kuri but any will do)
2–3 tbsp vegetable oil
¾ tsp and a pinch of sea salt
200 ml (7 fl oz/generous ¾ cup) coconut milk
200 ml (7 fl oz/generous ¾ cup) water

FOR THE REMPAH (SPICE PASTE)

100 g (3½ oz) shallots, roughly chopped
4 garlic cloves
thumb-sized piece (15 g/½ oz) fresh ginger, peeled and roughly chopped
3 large red chillies, roughly chopped
½ tsp ground turmeric
¼ tsp ground coriander

TO FINISH

juice of ½ lime
handful of fresh coriander (cilantro), roughly chopped
1 red chilli, thinly sliced (optional)

Preheat the oven to 210°C/190°C fan/410°F/gas mark 3.

Cut the squash into 2–3 cm (¾–1¼ in) wedges, removing any seeds and fibrous bits and leaving the skin on. Toss with the oil and a big pinch of sea salt and spread out on a large, deep roasting tray. Roast for 20 minutes.

In the meantime, pound all the spice paste ingredients using a pestle and mortar or whizz in a small blender until you get a fine paste. Fry the paste in a saucepan over medium heat until very fragrant, about 10 minutes. Stir in the coconut milk and water and bring to a simmer. Season with ¾ teaspoon of salt, or to taste.

Pour the sauce over the squash in the roasting tray, cover with foil, and continue to roast in the oven for another 20–25 minutes or until tender.

To serve, finish with a squeeze of lime, the chopped coriander and some chopped chilli, if you like.

SERVES 3–4

# Mamak Lentil Dal with Fried Curry Leaves

There is a street of casual open-air restaurants, just 10 minutes' walk away from my family home. Among them are two competing Mamak hawkers. I would go to the one that was open earlier on Sundays for breakfast and the one that shut later after a night out for supper. Whatever the time of the day, I would order *roti prata*, wonderfully greasy and flaky ghee flatbread that you dunk into a thin, spicy curry. It was a simple curry, made with lentils, curry leaves and maybe a few bits of tomato, but I would mop up every drop. This dal is a take on that hot, spicy *prata* curry. I've used more coconut and lentils to turn it into a richer dish that's perfect over plain steamed basmati rice.

1 tbsp vegetable oil
1 lemongrass stalk, bashed lightly
2 star anise
1 large onion, finely chopped
2 garlic cloves, finely chopped
1½ tbsp tomato purée (paste)
300 g (10½ oz) red lentils, soaked for 15 minutes then drained
400 ml (14 fl oz/generous 1½ cups) coconut milk
800 ml (27 fl oz/3¼ cups) water (see Tip)
1 tsp ground turmeric
1 tbsp lime juice
1¼ tsp fine sea salt, or to taste

TO FINISH

2 tbsp vegetable oil
1 tsp cumin seeds
2 green bird's eye chillies, halved lengthwise
10 fresh curry leaves

Heat 1 tablespoon of the oil in a large saucepan over medium heat. Once hot, add the lemongrass and star anise, followed by the onions. Fry until light golden, about 5 minutes. Then add the garlic and tomato purée, frying for another 2 minutes.

Tip in the lentils, coconut milk, water and turmeric.

Bring everything up to a boil, then cover and lower the heat so it cooks at a gentle simmer for 30 minutes. Stir once in a while so the dal doesn't stick to the bottom of the pan.

Fish out the lemongrass and star anise, then season the curry with the lime juice and salt, tasting and adjusting as you like.

Just before serving, in a separate small frying pan, heat the 2 tablespoons of oil to finish over high heat.

Now you want to work quickly so the spices don't burn! Add the cumin seeds, chillies and curry leaves to the hot oil, in that order. Once the curry leaves crackle, pour the spiced oil and fried curry leaves into the dal and stir through.

I like to fill up the empty coconut milk tin twice to measure out the water and rinse out the last of the coconut milk.

SERVES 3–4

# Tamil Egg Curry

There are many versions of egg curry; this is one I learnt from a Singaporean Indian friend, who in turn learnt and adapted it from her mum. The fennel seeds give an aniseed fragrance that's common to many Tamil curries, tomatoes and tamarind lend a sweet-sour tang, while the coconut milk (just a tiny drizzle!) adds a touch of creaminess. It's the perfect sauce to drench simple boiled eggs with. While runny yolks are very trendy, this is one recipe that calls for softer-set yolks to soak up that delicious curry sauce.

3–4 large eggs, room temperature (see Tip)
4 tbsp vegetable oil
1 tsp fennel seeds
1 small onion, finely sliced
thumb-sized (15 g/½ oz) piece of fresh ginger, peeled and finely chopped
2 medium ripe tomatoes, roughly chopped
1 tsp Kashmiri chilli powder
½ tsp ground turmeric
½ tsp ground coriander
¼ tsp ground cinnamon
1 tsp tamarind paste
4 tbsp coconut milk
10 fresh curry leaves
100 ml (3½ fl oz/scant ½ cup) water
½ tsp fine sea salt, or to taste
½ tsp light brown sugar, or to taste

Over medium–high heat, bring a saucepan of water to the boil. Carefully lower the eggs into the boiling water one at a time. Turn the heat down to a medium–low so the water is at a gentle boil/aggressive simmer, then cook for 8 minutes. When done, immediately transfer the eggs to a bowl of iced water to stop them cooking. Once the eggs are cool enough to hold, gently crack all over and peel, starting from the wider end, then cut in half. I like to leave the eggs chilling while I get the curry going.

Heat the oil in a large frying pan over medium heat. Add the fennel seeds and once they sizzle, tip in the onions and ginger. Fry until very fragrant and the onions turn a caramelised golden-brown.

Next, add the chopped tomatoes and fry, stirring often and crushing it slightly with your spatula, until they break down into a thick sauce. Add the spices and keep frying until the oil separates. Now, stir in the tamarind, coconut milk, curry leaves and the water. Season with salt and sugar and bring to a steady simmer.

Very gently slip the halved boiled eggs into the curry. Spoon the curry sauce over them, turn the heat off, and let the eggs soak up the flavours for a minute, or until you're ready to serve.

The fresher the eggs, the harder they are to peel. I like using old eggs for any recipe calling for boiled eggs to get a smooth peel.

# BROTHS A

**CHAPTER THREE**

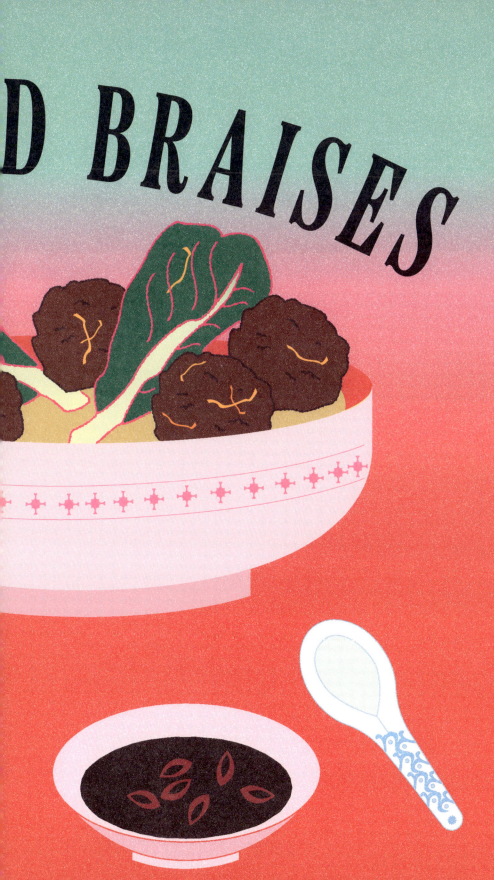

D BRAISES

CHAPTER THREE

# THREE

The recipes in this chapter all benefit from time.

It's not difficult to make a good broth or braise; it just requires a bit of patience. I liken the process to brewing a cup of tea – you need time for the leaves to sit and steep and infuse the liquid with flavour, but the wait is always worth it. There is nothing more bracing than a bowl of steaming broth; nothing more comforting than rice flooded with fragrant braising sauce.

For broths, I always start by blanching the meat and bones in boiling water, then I drain them and start again with fresh water and the spices or aromatics called for in the recipe. This reduces the amount of skimming you have to do to get a clear, 'clean' broth. The rest is pretty much effortless – you let the pot bubble away on the barest of heat. My mum used to leave her 'old-fire' broths over a low charcoal fire while she busied around the kitchen. In modern homes, a stove turned down low or a slow cooker will do the job nicely.

For braises, the idea is similar but you start by frying, rather than blanching, the meat or tofu. Once their edges brown and glisten, you stir in the seasonings and then, again, you let time do its clever thing. In fact, I love making braised meat dishes a day ahead. The flavours only meld and deepen overnight in the fridge. (If you're feeding guests, it also saves you a lot of panic on the day itself.)

Here, I've included traditional and new favourites, as well as a guide to basic stocks. The latter are always good to have in the fridge or freezer; you can always magic up quick, soothing dinners when you've got homemade stock.

# Basic Stock

Here's how you make an everyday stock that will work easily in all sorts of Singaporean recipes, from noodle soups to congee to jazzing up stir-fries. While you could add other bits and bobs for extra flavour, I've deliberately kept these stocks plain and versatile. The next few pages will show you how simmering the stock with sweet vegetables, or stirring in spice pastes and herbs like lemongrass can give you drastically different stock (broths), though the basic principles here mostly stay the same.

### Chicken or pork stock

Chicken or pork bones are most commonly used to make stock, particularly in Singaporean Chinese or Nonya cooking. Beef or lamb is considered too strongly flavoured. You could buy free-range chicken carcasses or stock bones from any good butcher for peanuts; or save the leftover bird from a roast; or if you plan on eating the meat, you could also use bone-on chicken legs or pork ribs.

Add 1 kg (2 lb 4 oz) of chicken or pork bones to a large pot of boiling water. Leave for a few minutes – you'll see icky scummy froth rising to the top. Drain and discard the cloudy water. Now return the rinsed bones to the pot and add enough water to cover, about 2 litres (68 fl oz/8½ cups). Bring to a boil, skimming off any more froth, though the first step should save you a fair bit of hovering around the stove. At this point you could add all sorts of vegetables, herbs and/or spices, but for an all-purpose stock I just add a knob of ginger and a few garlic cloves, left whole but bashed with the back of my knife. Then cover and simmer very gently for at least an hour, preferably longer. You can also do this in the slow cooker. This is all inactive time, so it really isn't a lot of effort at all. I sometimes have the leftover chicken carcass bubbling in the background while we're still eating our Sunday roast.

### Vegetarian stock

For a meat-free stock, you'll need to draw flavour out of vegetables that are naturally full of umami and sweetness. To 2 litres (68 fl oz/8½ cups) of water, I add an onion, two large carrots (or the same amount of mooli), one bunch of spring onions (scallions), a large handful of dried shiitake mushrooms, a knob of ginger and a few bashed garlic cloves. Bring to a boil, then cover, turn the heat down low and let simmer for an hour.

With either stock, strain when it's ready and season with about 2 teaspoons of fine sea salt, or to taste. It shouldn't be too salty as you want to be able to use it in a range of dishes. If you're not using the stock immediately, let it cool, then refrigerate and use it over the next few days, or portion and freeze it for rainy days.

### What about stock cubes?

While nothing beats a homemade stock, hands up I have reached for a quick stock cube on many, many occasions. If you do use one, just be mindful that they tend to be a bit saltier, so hold back on the seasoning and keep tasting! Most brands here also make use of Western herbs like rosemary and parsley, which can sometimes stand out in Asian cooking. I find Knorr's chicken powder or Kallo Organic's chicken/vegetarian umami stock cubes neutral enough, but always be ready to flavour-tweak with spices, fresh herbs and aromatics like ginger. For things like noodle soups, sometimes hot water stirred into Japanese miso paste may work better as a quick broth.

SERVES 3–4

# Soto Ayam with Spring Greens

While I mainly grew up with Mum's Chinese soups, I have fond memories of this Malay spiced chicken soup. My primary school canteen only had three stalls: one that sold tidbits; one that sold drinks; and one owned by a Malay Auntie with a daily changing special. My favourite dish was *soto ayam*: spiced chicken soup that's golden with turmeric and topped with fried shallots and mild sambal. It's mostly served with *lontong* (pressed rice cakes), fried potato cakes, rice noodles and/or hard-boiled eggs to make it more of a complete meal, but I often simply serve the flavour-packed broth with shredded chicken and vegetables as a side.

### FOR THE BROTH

750 g (1 lb 10 oz) chicken thighs or drumsticks, skin on and bone in
about 1½ litres (50¾ fl oz/ 6⅓ cups) water
1 lemongrass stalk, bashed lightly
1½ tsp fine sea salt, or to taste
2 tbsp vegetable oil
1 cinnamon bark
2 star anise

### FOR THE REMPAH (SPICE PASTE)

100 g (3½ oz) shallots, roughly chopped
thumb-sized piece (15 g/½ oz) fresh ginger, peeled and roughly chopped
2 garlic cloves
1 tbsp ground coriander
2 tsp ground cumin
1 tsp ground turmeric
1 tsp ground white pepper

### TO SERVE

bunch of spring greens, sliced into ribbons
juice of ½ lime, the remaining ½ sliced into wedges
handful of fresh coriander (cilantro), roughly chopped
1 spring onion (scallion), sliced thinly diagonally
Fried Shallots (page 209)
Sambal Tumis (page 204)

To a large pot filled with boiling water, add the chicken and cook for 3 minutes. Drain, discarding the scummy water. Now return the blanched chicken to the pot, cover with the measured fresh water and bring to the boil. Skim off and discard any scum that surfaces, then add the bruised lemongrass and salt, cover and simmer on low heat for 15 minutes.

While the stock is simmering, pound all the spice paste ingredients using a pestle and mortar or whizz in a small blender until you get a fine paste. If blending, you might need to add 1–2 tablespoons of water. Set a small frying pan over medium heat, with the vegetable oil. Once hot, add the cinnamon bark and star anise and fry for a minute until fragrant. Stir in the spice paste and keep frying for another 5 minutes before transferring the spice mix into the main stock pot.

Simmer the broth for 1 hour 30 minutes, then fish out the whole spices and remove the chicken. When cool enough to handle, tear the meat from the bones, shred into bite-sized pieces and divide among bowls.

Meanwhile, add the spring green ribbons to the bubbling broth and let cook, uncovered, until the greens wilt. Stir in the lime juice, then taste the broth at this stage and season with more salt as needed.

To serve, ladle the hot broth and spring greens into bowls with the shredded chicken. Top each bowl with the coriander, spring onion, and serve with the fried shallots, a dollop of sambal and the lime wedges.

SERVES 3–4

# Meatball Soup with Lettuce and Fried Ginger

When I want a soothing soup but don't have hours to wait, I make this. As the meatballs poach, they flavour the broth beautifully. At the very last minute, I add whatever greens I have to the hot broth. Here I use lettuce. This vegetable choice might seem unusual but I beg you to try it! The brief kiss of heat transforms the generic salad leaf into a very different beast – sweet, silky and tender.

### FOR THE MEATBALLS

250 g (9 oz) fatty minced (ground) pork
1 spring onion (scallion), finely chopped
1 tsp grated fresh ginger
½ tbsp light soy sauce
½ tsp sesame oil
¼ tsp fine sea salt
¼ tsp ground white pepper
1 tbsp cornflour (cornstarch)
1 tsp baking powder
about 3 tbsp cold water

### FOR THE BROTH

1 tbsp vegetable oil
30 g (1 oz) fresh ginger, cut into thin matchsticks
fine sea salt, to taste
about 1½ litres (50¾ fl oz/ 6 cups) water
4 tbsp fish sauce
¼ tsp ground white pepper
¼ tsp sesame oil

### TO SERVE

1 head of cos lettuce, roughly chopped into 5 cm (2 in) pieces
1 spring onion (scallion), finely chopped
Chilli Padi and Soy Sauce Dip (page 206)

NOTE

In a large mixing bowl, combine all the ingredients for the meatballs, except the water. Stir together in one direction. Add the cold water as you stir, a bit at a time, making sure the meat absorbs the liquid before adding more. Once the mixture comes together, pick it up with your hands and slam it down forcefully back into the bowl. Repeat until it becomes sticky and dense.

Now let's get the broth going. Heat the oil in a large pot set over medium heat. Add the ginger to the hot oil, with a pinch of salt. The ginger should sizzle straight away. Once golden brown, remove half the fried ginger with a slotted spoon and set aside for garnishing later.

Pour in the water, as well as the fish sauce, pepper and sesame oil, and bring to a gentle boil.

Form little balls with the meat mixture, squeezing and rolling to a compact round shape; don't worry if it's not smooth. Drop the meatballs straight into the simmering broth and cook until they all float to the surface. Then reduce the heat to low and let the meatballs simmer for another 10 minutes for their flavours to infuse the broth.

Now turn off the heat and stir in the lettuce, letting it wilt in the residual heat of the soup. Taste the soup at this stage, adjusting with more salt if you like.

Pour into bowls to serve and finish with the fried ginger and chopped spring onions as garnish. We also like to serve this with little saucers of dipping sauce – go for the simple and pumchy chilli padi and soy sauce dip.

Try changing up this soup by using Fried Garlic or Fried Shallots and their fragrant oils (page 209), instead of the fried ginger. You'll be surprised at how something so tiny can make such a huge difference to the flavour and fragrance of the soup!

SERVES 2–3

# ABC Sweetcorn, Carrot and Pork Rib Soup

I wanted to include this recipe as it's a perfect example of how simple it is to make a heavenly broth. You won't find ABC soup on the menu anywhere, but it's a dish that many Singaporean Chinese families will recognise and love. The origin of the name is fuzzy – some say it's as easy as ABC to make; others say it gives you all the essential vitamins A, B and C. The ingredients vary, but most versions will make use of pork ribs and naturally sweet vegetables: onions, carrot, sweetcorn and tomatoes.

500 g (1 lb 2 oz) pork ribs, cut into individual finger-length pieces
½ tsp fine sea salt, or to taste
about 1 litre (34 fl oz/4¼ cups) water
1 large onion, cut into quarters
1 corn on the cob, cut crosswise into 3 cm (1¼ in) rounds
1 large carrot, peeled and chopped into 2 cm (¾ in) chunks
1 tomato, cut into quarters
1 tbsp fish sauce

TO SERVE

2 tbsp Fried Garlic with Garlic Oil (page 209) (optional)
1 spring onion (scallion), finely chopped
Chilli Padi and Soy Sauce Dip (page 206)

To a large pot filled with boiling water, add the pork ribs and cook for 3 minutes. Drain, discarding the scummy water and rinsing the pork ribs under cold running water.

Now return the blanched pork to the pot, along with the salt and the measured fresh water, and bring to the boil. Skim off and discard any scum that surfaces, then cover and simmer on low heat for 30 minutes. Now add the vegetables and fish sauce and cook for another 30 minutes, or until the pork and vegetables are tender.

Taste the broth at this point, adding more salt if needed. The soup shouldn't be overly salty; you should be able to taste the light sweetness from the vegetables and pork.

To serve, ladle the soup into bowls, making sure to get a bit of the pork and vegetables. Finish with the crispy fried garlic and garlic oil, if using, and sprinkle the spring onions over. We also like to have little saucers of chilli padi and soy sauce dip on the side, for dipping the pork ribs into.

SERVES 4 GENEROUSLY, OR 8 AS A SIDE

# Teochew Braised Duck with Sweet Soy and Galangal

Days before a special family gathering, my Ah Ma (grandmother) would braise a whole duck. It's a dish that happily feeds the entire extended family, especially as eggs and/or tofu are often added as well. It's also a dish that really gets better with time, as the ingredients take on the flavours and beautiful dark colour of the braising sauce. A whole duck is usually used but I prefer using just duck legs; frying and flipping a large fatty bird is not for the faint-hearted.

4 duck legs (1 kg/2 lb 4 oz)
1 tsp coarse sea salt
2 tbsp five-spice powder
3 tbsp vegetable oil
30 g (1 oz) fresh galangal, peeled and sliced, or 2 tbsp galangal paste
30 g (1 oz) fresh ginger, peeled and sliced
6 garlic cloves, peeled and smashed
1 cinnamon bark
4 cloves
4 star anise
200 ml (7 fl oz/generous ¾ cup) dark soy sauce
2 tbsp kecap manis
2 tbsp light brown sugar
about 500 ml (17 fl oz/2 cups) water
4 large eggs, boiled for 7 minutes and peeled

TO SERVE

plain steamed rice
sliced cucumber
handful of coriander (cilantro)
Garlic Chilli Sauce (page 206)

Rub the duck legs with the salt and five-spice powder.

Heat the vegetable oil in a wide casserole pot (Dutch oven) set over medium heat. Add the duck legs, skin-side down, and turn the heat down to low. Leave the duck legs to fry – no need to poke! – until the skin turns golden and the fat is rendered, about 10 minutes. Remove from the pot and set aside.

Now fry the galangal, ginger, garlic, cinnamon, cloves and star anise in the rendered duck fat until very fragrant, about 5 minutes. If using galangal paste instead of fresh galangal slices, add it a little later so it doesn't burn.

Return the duck legs to the pot and stir in the dark soy sauce, kecap manis, sugar and enough water to submerge the duck legs. Bring to a boil, cover, then reduce the heat to low. Let simmer, covered, for 2 hours 30 minutes, until the meat is very tender. (Or pressure-cook on High for 30 minutes.)

Turn off the heat and add the whole boiled eggs to the pot. Cover and leave for at least 2 hours at room temperature or, even better, overnight in the fridge. This will really make sure the duck legs and eggs are infused with the flavour of the braising sauce.

Warm everything back up when you are ready to serve. This is best served with plain steamed rice to soak up the braising sauce, as well as cucumber, coriander and garlic chilli sauce.

TIP

This recipe makes plenty of braising sauce. Any leftover sauce can be poured through a sieve (fine mesh strainer) into a Tupperware box and then frozen, to be added to the next braise. This makes each braise that you make more and more flavourful with time. In fact, the most famous hawkers pride themselves on the age of their braising sauce.

SERVES 3–4

# Mum's Soy-Braised Pork Belly and Shiitake Mushrooms

*Tau yew bak* is a weekly must-have at the Lee family dinner table. As with many braises, this is a dish that only tastes better the next day. It was ideal for my busy mum; she could make a big pot and reheat it the next day alongside some simple stir-fried vegetables for dinner. Slow braising turns the cheap cut of meat into a delicious, meltingly soft thing and the resulting sauce is rich with flavour, ideal for drenching plain rice with. The dried shiitake mushrooms are my favourite part; they rehydrate by soaking up the braising sauce, becoming plump with flavour.

2 star anise
1 tbsp white peppercorns
1 cinnamon bark
2 tbsp vegetable oil
1 bulb of garlic, peeled and smashed
500 g (1 lb 2 oz) pork belly, cut into 3 cm (1¼ in) large chunks
1½ tbsp light brown sugar
100 ml (3½ fl oz/scant ½ cup) dark soy sauce
3 tbsp rice wine
8 dried shiitake mushrooms, stems broken off and discarded
about 500 ml (17 fl oz/2 cups) water
plain steamed rice, to serve

In a wok or wide casserole pot set over medium–low heat, toast the spices until fragrant, then remove and set aside.

Turn the heat up to medium and add the oil. Once hot, fry the garlic until fragrant, before pushing to the side of the wok or pot. Add the pork and sugar and fry, stirring occasionally, until the meat turns golden and glossy.

Now add the rest of the ingredients to the pot, including the toasted spices from earlier, with just enough of the water to cover the pork. Bring everything to a gentle boil before covering and turning the heat down to low. Let simmer for 2 hours until the pork is very tender. (Or pressure-cook on High for 30 minutes.)

Make sure you have plenty of plain steamed rice to serve this with, as you will want to drench it with this braising sauce.

This braising sauce is a versatile one that goes not just with pork. Replace with chicken legs and/or tofu – extra-firm tofu blocks or dried tofu knots.

SERVES 3–4

# Chicken Braised in Tamarind and Coriander

*Ayam sio* is a delicious example of how early Nonya cooks have adapted classic Chinese soy braises with local spices like coriander seed, and fruits like tamarind. The tangy sauce is incredibly more-ish and it works especially well with fattier meats like duck and pork belly. For a more everyday version, I use chicken with skin on and bone in, as always with a braise.

750 g (1 lb 10 oz) chicken drumsticks, skin on and bone in
2 tbsp ground coriander
1 tsp white pepper
big pinch of coarse sea salt
3 tbsp vegetable oil
200 g (7 oz) shallots, roughly chopped
2 tbsp dark soy sauce
4 tbsp tamarind paste
1 tbsp white rice vinegar, or apple cider vinegar
2 tbsp soft light brown sugar, or to taste
1 tsp fine sea salt, or to taste
about 500 ml (17 fl oz/2 cups) water

TO FINISH

½ red chilli, thinly sliced
few sprigs of fresh coriander (cilantro)

Rub the chicken with the ground coriander, white pepper and coarse sea salt. Set aside to marinate while you prepare the shallots – simply pound them using a pestle and mortar or whizz in a small blender to a fine paste.

Heat the vegetable oil in a wide casserole pot (Dutch oven) set over medium heat. Add the chicken skin-side down and fry until browned, then flip over and do the same so they colour all over. Remove from the pot and set aside.

Tip in the shallots and fry until fragrant and light golden. Now stir in the rest of the ingredients and return the chicken to the pot, adding just enough water to cover the chicken.

Bring everything to a gentle boil before covering and turning the heat down to low. Let simmer, partially covered, for about an hour, or until the chicken is tender. Remove the lid and let the sauce reduce to a rich, thick consistency, spooning it over the chicken occasionally to keep the meat moist while doing so.

Finally, taste and adjust seasoning with a touch more salt or sugar if you like, then garnish with the chilli and coriander.

SERVES 3–4 AS A SIDE

# Braised Egg Tofu with Mushrooms and Sugar Snaps

Egg tofu is a special kind of tofu made from soy milk and eggs – the eggs giving it a wobbly, pudding-like texture. It's set in a tube and is just firm enough to hold its shape in the pan, making it perfect for braised dishes. This recipe is inspired by one of my favourite *tze char* dishes while growing up – *tie ban dou fu*, or hotplate tofu. Egg tofu is sliced and fried to get beautiful golden-yellow rounds, then scattered over beaten egg and smothered in a rich savoury sauce made of minced (ground) pork and mushrooms. This was brought to the table in a sizzling hotplate, so the dish would still be bubbling and cooking right in front of you. The waiter would shout '*sio!*' (hot), and all the children would jump away, squealing with delight. This is a simpler version of that childhood favourite, with a bit less theatre but all the flavour.

6 dried shiitake mushrooms
500 ml (17 fl oz/2 cups) hot water
1 tbsp light soy sauce
2 tbsp dark soy sauce
2 tbsp oyster sauce
2 x 150 g (5½ oz) tubes of egg tofu (see Note)
vegetable oil, for frying
pinch of fine sea salt
thumb-sized piece (15 g/½ oz) fresh ginger, peeled and finely chopped
2 garlic cloves, finely chopped
200 g (7 oz) fatty minced (ground) pork
2 tbsp taucheo
1 tsp sesame oil
2 large red chillies, thinly sliced
100 g (3½ oz) sugar snap peas or mangetout (snow peas)
1 tbsp cornflour (cornstarch), stirred into 3 tbsp cold water

Rinse and soak the dried shiitake mushrooms in the hot water until they are soft and plump, before draining (reserve the soaking water) and slicing thinly. Into the soaking liquid, stir the light soy sauce, dark soy sauce and oyster sauce. This will form our braising sauce for later.

While the mushrooms are soaking, slice the egg tofu into 2 cm (¾ in) thick rounds and pat dry. Heat ½ cm (¼ in) of oil in a large frying pan, set over medium heat. Add the tofu in a single layer, sprinkle with a pinch of salt and fry until golden, then flip over and do the same on the other side. Set aside on kitchen paper (paper towels) to drain, leaving a couple tablespoons of oil in the pan.

Add the ginger and garlic, frying for a few seconds until fragrant. Now turn up the heat, add the pork and spread out so it browns evenly. Once golden brown and cooked, stir-fry with the sliced shiitake mushrooms, taucheo and sesame oil for a minute or so. Pour in the mushroom braising sauce, scraping to deglaze any browned bits in the pan. Once the sauce is bubbling, return the egg tofu to the pan along with the chillies and sugar snap peas or mangetout. Cover and turn the heat down low until the greens are just cooked – bright green but still crisp.

Remove the lid and slowly add the cornflour slurry, stirring it gently through the sauce. I like to add just half the cornflour slurry, then add more as needed. Let simmer for a minute or so until the sauce thickens to your liking. Serve piping hot.

NOTE

Egg tofu can be found in most Asian supermarkets, alongside the fresh chilled tofu. If you can't get hold of it, you can use medium-firm tofu instead.

TIP

To turn this into a vegetarian dish, replace the minced pork with 200 g (7 oz) minced chestnut mushrooms, and the oyster sauce with a vegetarian mushroom 'oyster' sauce.

# STIR-FRY SIMPLE

## CHAPTER FOUR

# ...IES AND SIDES

## CHAPTER FOUR

# FOUR

Many young Singaporeans today don't cook because cheap, tasty food is so easily available in hawker centres or casual restaurants. Funnily, I really only learnt to cook when I moved *away* from Singapore and was homesick for the food I had taken for granted. I remember the first meals I cooked for myself – two fried eggs, chopped cucumber, undercooked rice, lots of soy sauce to 'tie it all together'. I also remember being very proud of myself as I chewed on the dry, hard grains.

Now I cook almost every day. Even after a long day or late night, I look first in the fridge before I give in to the call of the takeaway (takeout). Often, there are just enough eggs for an omelette; the ends of vegetables to throw together in a stir-fry with oyster sauce. Then you just need to pop the rice cooker on while you're in the shower and dinner's in the bag.

Once you get into the habit of cooking, you will find it easier and more satisfying to rustle up something delicious. It doesn't have to be long or fussy. While I love spending time in the kitchen, the realities of life mean that the sort of things I cook most often take hardly any time at all. This chapter is full of the recipes I cook regularly; some are classics, others are dreamed up in moments of desperation. Every one has a short and simple list of ingredients – all you need are storecupboard staples or the handy make-ahead sauces from the last chapter.

SERVES 2–3 AS A SIDE

# Soy Sauce and Ketchup Prawns

This recipe is a tribute to my mother-in-law, Debbie, who's suffered plenty of jabs from her son about her attempts at cooking Chinese food in his childhood. 'Noodles with soy sauce and ketchup!' The combination actually sounded brilliant to me the first time I heard about it. In fact, tomato ketchup features quite often in Singaporean dishes, not just as a condiment but as a cooking ingredient. Singaporean food is often about bringing together sweet, salty and sour flavours, and ketchup is all of those in a perfectly balanced bottle, so it's no wonder cooks have taken to it. Here, it's stir-fried together with the usual Chinese aromatics and sweet king prawns (shrimp).

350 g (12 oz) raw jumbo king prawns (shrimp), peeled, tails on
3 tbsp vegetable oil
thumb-sized piece of fresh ginger, peeled and sliced into matchsticks
2 garlic cloves, sliced thinly
2 spring onions (scallions), sliced diagonally, white and green parts separated
4 tbsp tomato ketchup
2 tbsp Shaoxing rice wine
2 tbsp light soy sauce, or to taste
1 red bird's eye chilli, finely chopped

Use a sharp knife or kitchen scissors to cut down the back of each prawn from the head to just before the tail, then lift out the black line with the tip of your knife and pull to remove. This not only deveins the prawn but helps it to open up into a beautiful butterfly shape when fried later. Pat dry with kitchen paper (paper towels).

Add half the oil to a wok or large frying pan set over high heat. Once smoking hot, add the prawns in a single layer. Fry until they turn orange and char on the edges, then flip over and do the same on the other side. Remove and set aside; the prawns won't be fully cooked through at this stage, but don't worry, we'll return them to the wok later.

Turn the heat down to low. Add the remaining oil, ginger, garlic and white parts of the spring onions to the remaining oil in the wok or pan. Let them sizzle gently and infuse the oil for 10 seconds.

Turn the heat back up to a medium–high heat, stir in the chilli and seasonings, and quickly stir-fry for a minute. Return the fried prawns to the pan, gently stirring until the sauce reduces and coats the prawns.

Finally, finish with the green parts of the spring onion, give everything one last toss in the wok or pan, before dishing out to serve.

SERVES 2–3

# Oyster Sauce Sweetheart Cabbage

Greens stir-fried with oyster sauce is a very common dish served both at home and at *tze char* stalls. I'm of the strong belief that no vegetable can taste bad with this combination of fragrant garlic and rich, salty oyster sauce. I've used cabbage here just to prove my point – a vegetable that many people seem to turn their noses up at. The other important trick (as with most green vegetables) is not to overcook it, so it keeps its crisp texture and sweetness.

1 pointed (sweetheart) cabbage
8 garlic cloves, unpeeled
2 tbsp vegetable oil
2 tbsp oyster sauce (see Note)
1 tsp light soy sauce
1 tsp of light brown sugar
splash of water (about 3–4 tbsp)

Halve the pointed cabbage lengthwise, remove the core, and cut into 3 cm (1¼ in) large pieces. Smash the garlic with the flat side of your knife, but I like to leave them whole in their skins. This helps them not to burn as easily, plus I get the bonus of sweet roasted garlic cloves.

Heat the oil in a wok or a large frying pan over medium heat. Add the garlic and stir-fry until fragrant and lightly golden.

Turn the heat up to high and add the cabbage. Stir-fry until wilted and tender, but still crisp, about 3 minutes.

Stir in the oyster sauce, soy sauce and sugar and continue stir-frying for 30 seconds. Add a splash of water to deglaze any browned bits, bring to a simmer and cook until the liquid has reduced slightly, about 2 minutes. Serve immediately.

For vegans, this recipe works just as well with 'oyster' sauce alternatives. The latter sauce is often made with mushrooms instead of oysters for savoury depth and is labelled as 'vegetarian stir-fry sauce'.

SERVES 2–3 AS A SIDE

# Rainbow Chard Belacan

*Kangkong belacan* is one of Singapore's favourite vegetable side dishes. It's a simple dish of water spinach stir-fried with shrimp paste and chilli. You will find it served at Chinese *tze char* places, Malay *nasi padang* stalls, Nonya restaurants, and in the homes of many Singaporeans. Beyond our love for everything pungent and spicy, what makes this dish special is the contrast of crunchy stalks and silky smooth leaves. Here in the UK, I find chard to be a worthy equivalent of *kangkong*, and if you can get hold of the candy-coloured rainbow chard, it turns this dish into a real feast for the eyes, too.

300 g (10½ oz) rainbow chard or Swiss chard
2 tbsp dried shrimps, soaked in 3 tbsp hot water until softened
2 tsp belacan (fermented shrimp paste)
3 garlic cloves
1 banana shallot, roughly chopped
1 tbsp groundnut oil
2 bird's eye chillies, finely chopped
¼ tsp light brown sugar
big pinch of fine sea salt, to taste

Separate the chard stalks from the leaves. Cut the stalks into batons and roughly shred the leaves.

Pound the dried shrimp, belacan, garlic and shallot together using a pestle and mortar or whizz in a small blender until you get a rough paste, adding the hot soaking water to help dissolve the belacan.

Set a wok over medium heat and add the oil. When hot, add the spice paste and fry for 5 minutes until very fragrant, stirring often.

Now turn up the heat. Add the chard stalks and chopped chillies to the wok and stir-fry for 2 minutes until softened, before adding the leaves. Season with sugar and a big pinch of salt and stir-fry until the leaves are completely wilted. Taste and adjust with more salt if necessary – both the dried shrimp and shrimp paste are salty so you might not find you need more.

Plate up and eat straight away.

If you have a jar of Sambal Belacan (page 205) in the fridge already, you can do an even quicker variation of this recipe. Simply fry 2 tablespoons of the sambal with the chopped shallots and soaked dried shrimps, then chuck your greens into the wok with the soaking water and season to taste.

SERVES 2–3 AS A SIDE

# Green Beans with Turmeric and Toasted Coconut

This simple vegetable side brings together all my favourite flavours and smells: the nuttiness of toasted coconut, the vibrance of turmeric and the fresh sharpness of lime. I also chuck in fried shallots and fragrant shallot oil when I have them in my pantry, as they take the dish to a whole different level! I've used green beans here but feel free to replace them with any crisp green vegetable and adjust the cooking times accordingly.

400 g (14 oz) fine green beans, tails removed
4 heaped tbsp desiccated (shredded) coconut
½ tsp fine sea salt, or to taste
2 tbsp extra virgin coconut oil, or Fried Shallot Oil (page 209)
½ tsp ground turmeric
1 red bird's eye chilli, sliced
juice of ½ lime (about 1 tbsp)
2 tbsp Fried Shallots (page 209) (optional)

Put a saucepan of water on to boil and cook the beans until tender but still crisp to bite into, about 3 minutes. Drain and leave to dry.

Meanwhile, set a dry frying pan over medium heat. Add the desiccated coconut and half the salt to the pan, shaking and stirring often so it doesn't burn. Remove the toasted coconut and set aside just as it turns a pale golden, because it will continue cooking to a golden brown off the heat.

Now, add the oil to the pan and then turn the heat to low. Stir in the turmeric and chilli, cooking for about 30 seconds so they infuse the oil. Add the green beans and remaining salt to the frying pan and toss to combine. Squeeze the lime juice over and, once everything is sizzling, stir in most of the toasted coconut.

Taste and adjust seasoning as needed before serving. Finish by sprinkling over the rest of the toasted coconut and fried shallots, if using.

SERVES 3–4

# Cucumber, Pineapple and Peanut Rojak with Tamarind Dressing

This is a salad very loosely inspired by the Singaporean 'rojak', an eclectic salad of crunchy fruit and vegetables, drenched in a dressing made of *hei ko*, a dark and gooey sweet shrimp paste. I've kept all the elements I love about it here: crisp cucumber, juicy pineapple, aromatic roasted peanuts and a sweet fruity dressing. The tamarind, lime and chilli dressing is key to bringing this salad together. It's fresh and zesty, with just enough heat for it to tingle on your tongue. It's also versatile enough to work with all sorts of vegetables, so feel free to double it and use it to liven up any boring salad.

1 large cucumber
250 g (9 oz) pineapple, peeled, seeds and eyes removed
½ small red onion, very finely chopped
50 g (1¾ oz) freshly roasted peanuts, crushed
handful of mint leaves, roughly chopped

### FOR THE DRESSING

4 tbsp tamarind paste
4 tbsp lime juice
2 tbsp light brown sugar
¾ tsp fine sea salt
1 bird's eye chilli, finely chopped

Combine the ingredients for the dressing, stirring to dissolve the sugar and salt.

Quarter the cucumber lengthwise, cut off the seedy middle, then cut into 1 cm (½ in) pieces. Cut the pineapple into similar-sized pieces.

Mix the cucumber, pineapple and red onion together with the dressing. Set aside for 5 minutes.

When ready to serve, add the peanuts and mint and toss to combine.

SERVES 2-3 AS A SIDE

# Steamed Asparagus with Garlicky Black Bean Sauce

I discovered the bittersweet, earthy joys of asparagus when I moved to the UK and now I, too, look forward to the few weeks of the year when the bright green spears are in season. British chefs treat asparagus with a sort of reverence, giving it the most straightforward treatment: steaming or blanching until just done, then serving with nothing more than melted butter and sea salt. I agree simple is best, but after a week of purist asparagus eating, I like to branch out. This recipe is just a step on from the classic approach. Instead of butter, I dress the steamed asparagus with a warm garlicky black bean sauce.

300 g (10½ oz) asparagus
2 tbsp vegetable oil
4 garlic cloves, finely sliced
2 tsp salted black beans, rinsed and finely chopped
1 red chilli, finely chopped
1 tsp light soy sauce
1 tsp sesame oil
about 2 tbsp water

Trim off any woody ends from the asparagus and place the stems in a steamer basket, set over gently boiling water. Cover and steam over medium heat for 2–4 minutes, depending on the thickness of the spears, until bright green and tender but still crisp.

Meanwhile, prepare the sauce. In a small frying pan, heat the oil over medium heat. Add the sliced garlic to the hot oil; the garlic should sizzle steadily. After a minute, add the salted black beans and chilli and fry. Keep stirring until the garlic turns golden and the mixture is very fragrant.

Now, stir in the light soy sauce, sesame oil and 2 tablespoons of water, and bring everything to a simmer.

When the asparagus is done, pour the hot fragrant sauce all over and serve.

SERVES 2

# Shu's Spicy Late Night Special

This was concocted in a moment of desperation, but it has since saved me on many hungry late nights when the takeaway options are dire. This five-minute stir-fry makes use of a simple ingredient found in most fridges – minced (ground) meat – and is finished with whatever fresh fragrant herbs you have lying around. I've purposely left out the usual chopped garlic, ginger or shallots found at the start of a stir-fry, because these are *not* the sort of nights for peeling and chopping. Instead, the dish packs a punch with a few storecupboard staple seasonings, garlic oil (if you have it) and bird's eye chilli – snipped straight into the wok with kitchen scissors.

2 tbsp vegetable oil or Garlic Oil (page 209)
250 g (9 oz) fatty minced (ground) pork
2 tbsp oyster sauce
1 tsp fish sauce
1 tsp light brown sugar
100 g (3½ oz) frozen peas
1 fresh or frozen red bird's eye chilli (see Tip)
3–4 tbsp water
large handful (20 g/¾ oz) of fresh coriander (cilantro), Thai basil and/or basil
plain rice or blanched noodles, to serve

Heat the oil in a wok or a large frying pan over high heat. When smoking hot, add the pork, using your spatula to break up the meat and distribute over the base of the wok or pan. Leave the pork to fry, untouched, until it browns.

Once the pork turns golden brown at the edges, let the action begin! Add the oyster sauce, fish sauce and sugar and keep stirring and frying for a couple of minutes.

Chuck in the frozen peas. Using kitchen scissors, snip the chilli directly into the wok. Keep stirring until the peas turn bright green and tender and the pork is cooked through. Add a little splash of water – just enough to form a sauce – and bring to a simmer for 30 seconds.

Remove the wok from the heat. Roughly tear the herbs and gently fold them into the meat until they wilt from the residual heat in the wok. Serve immediately over plain rice or blanched noodles.

I like to stick my bird's eye chillies straight into the freezer so I have a steady supply of them; they freeze beautifully. To use, simply hold the frozen chilli under a running tap for a minute. Once softened, you can chop (or snip!) away.

# Steamed Egg Custard

SERVES 2

This is a Chinese household favourite that many of us would have grown up with. A good steamed egg is soft and delicate with a smooth surface, kind of like a savoury set custard – so it's no wonder it's a favourite among the children. My mum almost always uses the same shallow dish for steaming eggs in … not just for luck, but because she can then 'measure' the right amount of stock to add to her eggs. She has an alternative genius trick for when she doesn't have her favourite dish at hand: she uses eggshell halves as measuring cups, so she doesn't have to remember numbers or worry about the size of eggs.

2 large free-range eggs
6 eggshell-halves (about 135 ml/4½ fl oz) of cold water or chicken/vegetable stock (broth)
½ tsp Shaoxing rice wine
pinch of fine sea salt
pinch of ground white pepper

TO SERVE

1 spring onion (scallion), finely sliced diagonally
1 tbsp groundnut oil
½ tsp toasted sesame oil
2 tsp light soy sauce, or to taste

Beat the eggs well with the water or stock, rice wine, salt and pepper. Strain the mixture through a sieve (fine mesh strainer) to get rid of the bubbles into a shallow (about 2 cm (¾ in) high) heatproof dish that will fit over a saucepan. Seal the dish with foil or cling film (plastic wrap).

Prepare your steamer: bring a pan of water to a boil, then set the dish over the top, making sure the bottom of the dish isn't touching the water. Cover, turn the heat down and steam on medium heat for 15 minutes or until set. If you're not sure, shake the dish a little; it should be jiggly but firm.

To serve, sprinkle the spring onions on top of the steamed eggs. Heat the oils until smoking hot, pour over the eggs, then drizzle the soy sauce over. The hot oil scalds the spring onions to release their fragrance and allows the soy sauce to glide smoothly over the whole dish. Adjust the soy sauce according to taste – you may need less if you used a seasoned stock.

SERVES 1–2

# Fish Sauce Omelette

An omelette is one of the first things I learnt to make as a starving student, and it's still one of the things I love to make regularly – not just for breakfasts, but for quick lunches and dinners. The one I grew up with is fluffy on the inside and golden brown on the outside, and seasoned with soy or fish sauce rather than salt for extra flavour. I also like to chuck in whatever herbs are available.

2 large free-range eggs
1 tsp fish sauce, or to taste (see Tip)
¼ tsp ground white pepper
2 tbsp vegetable oil
1 spring onion (scallion), finely chopped, white and green parts separated
½ red chilli, finely chopped
handful of fresh herbs, such as coriander (cilantro), mint or Thai basil

Beat the eggs in a bowl with the fish sauce and white pepper.

Heat a small frying pan set over medium–high heat. Add the oil and, when hot, fry the white parts of the spring onions and the chopped chilli for a few seconds until fragrant.

Pour in the beaten eggs – they should sizzle immediately in the hot oil. Let the egg set slightly before using a spatula or pair of chopsticks to push the cooked sides of the omelette into the centre and swirling the pan so the raw egg runs to the edges. Do this until the egg is mostly cooked and golden brown underneath. It's ok for the middle to be a bit runny.

Sprinkle the herbs and green parts of the spring onions on top before folding or flipping. Let cook for a few seconds more before dishing up. You can serve this whole, folded in half or snipped into pieces to scatter over dishes like Plain Congee (page 36) or Hot Smoked Mackerel and Ginger Congee (page 156).

TIP

I like my omelettes saltier to serve alongside plain rice or congee. If you're having this on its own, use a touch less fish sauce. To make this vegan-friendly, you can use light soy sauce instead.

SERVES 1–2 AS A SIDE

# Fried Egg Tempra with Onions and Kecap Manis

*Tempra* refers to the method of braising onions with sweet soy sauce. Chilli is added for heat, and lime for a refreshing tang. The simple ingredients transform into a sticky, zingy, caramel-like sauce. It's a sauce that's glorious spooned over anything and everything – in this instance (and in many other hungry instances), fried eggs.

3 tbsp vegetable oil
2 large free-range eggs
1 small onion, sliced into ½ cm (¼ in) thick rounds
1–2 bird's eye chillies, cut in half lengthwise
1 tbsp dark soy sauce
1 tbsp kecap manis
about 2 tbsp water
juice of ½ lime
2 sprigs of fresh coriander (cilantro)

Heat the oil in a small frying pan set over medium–high heat. Crack the eggs into the hot oil – you should see the oil bubbling around the whites from the start. Fry until the whites turn lacy and golden brown on the edges and are set around the yolk – you might want to spoon the hot oil over the whites to help them set. Remove the eggs from the pan with a spatula and set aside on your serving plate.

Add the sliced onions to the remaining oil in the pan and fry until fragrant and golden. Now add the chillies, soy sauce, kecap manis and a small splash of the water to help deglaze the pan. Once bubbling, add a squeeze of lime juice, stir through, then pour the sauce over the fried eggs. Tear the coriander over to garnish and serve immediately.

SERVES 2 AS A SIDE

# Silken Tofu with Salted Black Beans and Spring Onion

This is the dish I like to make for those who claim they don't like tofu. Unlike the more widely known firm tofu, silken tofu has a custard-like texture and a mild, creamy flavour that takes well to all sorts of delicious dressings and sauces. Because it's so soft, silken tofu isn't best suited for frying or tossing around in the wok. I like to have it raw, smothered with this fragrant, pungent black bean sauce.

1 block (300 g/10½ oz) of silken tofu, drained
1 tbsp vegetable oil
1 tbsp salted black beans, rinsed briefly and finely chopped
1 garlic clove, finely chopped
5 g (¼ oz) fresh ginger, peeled and finely chopped
1 tbsp dark soy sauce
½ tsp sugar
1 tsp chilli oil or sesame oil (depending on spice preference)
about 1 tbsp water
2 spring onions (scallions), finely sliced diagonally, white and green parts separated

Very carefully slide the silken tofu out of its packaging onto a plate. Slice into 2 cm (¾ in) thick slices, fanning them out so they overlap each other slightly.

To prepare the sauce, heat the oil over high heat in a small frying pan. Add the salted black beans, garlic and ginger to the hot oil and stir-fry for 30 seconds until very fragrant. Add in the white parts of the spring onion and let sizzle for another 10 seconds. Stir in the soy sauce, sugar, your choice of flavoured oil and an extra tablespoon of water. Bring everything to a simmer.

Pour the hot black bean sauce over the tofu and finish with the green parts of the spring onions.

STIR-FRIES AND SIMPLE SIDES

# FOOD FOR

## CHAPTER FIVE

# FEASTING

## CHAPTER FIVE

# FIVE

In Singapore, food is an excuse to gather. I happen to be writing this section over the Lunar New Year holidays in Singapore and I'm reminded just how much we love a feast. There has been a steady stream of potlucks and hotpots, with Aunts and Uncles and primary school friends whom I haven't seen in years. My mum has spent the last week preparing for our family reunion dinner – waking up at 5am to seize the freshest crabs from the market, rolling *ngoh hiang* (five-spice pork rolls), marinating meats in soy and rice wine and soaking nuts and seeds for sweet soups.

I have always enjoyed the eating of a feast (no surprise), but once I started cooking for others I understood the joy of preparing one, too. I love the whole process – from pondering over a menu before the day, to rolling my guests home at the end of the night. I love watching their faces as they take their first bite and hearing the thoughts and stories that unfold after. I love feeding people – whether they're old friends or strangers coming together for the first time at my supper club.

My parents have never been ones to freely say 'I love you', but I know that a table aching with plates of my favourite things means just that. Feeding is very much our love language; to feed is to show you care. As such, the best feasts are never about the most expensive, extravagant dishes, but the care that the cooks put in. In this chapter, you'll find sharing dishes that look and feel a bit more special. They may require a little more time and/or effort, but none of them are difficult to make and the results are always worth it.

**NOTE**

When hosting a feast, it's important to make sure the hosts (you) are having fun and not stressing out, with too much work on your hands. Don't create a menu made up only of dishes from this chapter! I like to combine a few of the more show-stopping dishes here with simpler sides or make-ahead curries and braises from the other chapters.

SERVES 4–6

# Salt and Pepper Crispy Roast Pork Belly

Roast pork belly is an absolute crowd pleaser and when done right it needs nothing more than just salt and pepper to flavour it. This is my time-tested method for salty, crispy crackling and juicy, tender meat. While impressive looking, it takes hardly any effort and the three-hour slow roast is pretty much all idle time – perfect for getting all the other bits of your feast ready (and maybe even to kick back with a cup of tea).

1.5 kg (3 lb 5 oz) piece of boneless pork belly, skin on
1 tbsp coarse sea salt and a pinch more
2 tsp ground white pepper
1 tbsp vegetable oil

Using a very sharp knife, score the skin of the pork. You want to cut into the skin and fat but not the meat, or else the juices run as the pork cooks and lead to soggy crackling. Alternatively, get your friendly butcher to do that for you.

The other key step for crispy crackling is to make sure the pork belly is very dry. If you have time, leave it uncovered in the fridge overnight. Otherwise, just pat dry with kitchen paper (paper towels) and give it a short blast with a hairdryer.

When ready to cook, lay the pork belly on a rack set skin-side up over a roasting tray, cover and leave until the pork belly comes to room temperature. Meanwhile, preheat the oven to 220°C/200°C fan/425°F/gas mark 7. Stir together the salt, pepper and oil and rub this seasoning all over the pork, making sure to really rub it in.

Roast for 30 minutes, before reducing the heat to 180°C/160°C fan/350°F/gas mark 4 and roasting for a further 2 hours 30 minutes.

To finish the crackling, sprinkle a pinch more sea salt over the skin, then whack the heat up on the grill (broiler) setting. Cook for another few minutes, just until the skin turns golden brown and very crisp. Keep an eye on it, as it's easy to burn the crackling at this stage! Depending on your oven, you might even find you don't need this extra step for golden, crispy crackling.

Remove the pork from the oven and leave to rest for at least 20 minutes before cutting into pieces. The longer you leave it, the juicier the meat and the easier it is to get neat slices à la a traditional Cantonese roast meats hawker.

SERVES 4

# Cereal Prawns with Butter and Curry Leaves

This is a clever recipe thought up by the creative *tze char* chefs of Singapore, bringing together Chinese, Indian and Western techniques and ingredients. Prawns (shrimps) are fried until golden, then tossed in butter with chilli, curry leaves and … instant cereal. It sounds like a crazy combination, but it works. It's sweet, salty, buttery and incredibly fragrant. I've yet to leave a plate unfinished – not even a single crumb of toasted cereal. The original dish uses Nestum, a Malaysian brand of fortified mixed grain cereal. Here I've used British instant oats – you want oat flakes instead of rolled oats here so they toast quickly and coat the fried prawns easily.

350 g (12 oz) raw jumbo king prawns (shrimps), peeled, tails on
1 tsp fine sea salt, or to taste
¼ tsp ground white pepper
2 tbsp plain (all-purpose) flour
2 tbsp vegetable oil
10 curry leaves
2 red bird's eye chillies, halved
1 tbsp unsalted butter
50 g (1¾ oz) plain instant oats (oatmeal)
1½ tsp light brown sugar, or to taste

Use a sharp knife or kitchen scissors to cut down the back of each prawn from the head to just before the tail, then lift out the black line with the tip of your knife and pull to remove. This not only deveins the prawn but helps it to open up into a beautiful butterfly shape when fried later. Pat dry with kitchen paper (paper towels), then toss the prawns with ¾ teaspoon of salt, the white pepper and flour.

Add the oil to a wok or large frying pan set over high heat. Once smoking hot, add the prawns in a single layer. Fry until they turn orange and char on the edges, then flip over and do the same on the other side. The prawns should be about 90 per cent cooked at this point, as we'll be returning the prawns to the pan later. Remove and set aside, keeping the seafood-flavoured oil in the pan.

Turn the heat down to medium, add the curry leaves and chillies to the hot oil and fry until the leaves crackle. Then add the butter, oats, remaining salt and the sugar, toasting for 3–5 minutes or until golden and fragrant. Taste and season with more salt or sugar if you like. Now return the prawns to the pan and toss well to coat, for another half a minute.

Dish out and serve straight away, making sure to get every last bit of that addictive cereal crumb onto the plate.

SERVES 4

# Nonya Lemongrass Roast Chicken

If I had to pick my favourite British food, the humble roast chicken would definitely be one of my top contenders. I love everything about roast chicken – the homely smell that permeates the kitchen as it cooks in the oven, the theatre of bringing a whole bird to the table and carving it to share, the delicious contrast of crisp brown skin and juicy meat. This chicken dish brings together the best of both worlds: the classic British roast chicken and the fragrant Peranakan *ayam panggang* (grilled spiced chicken). The sweet coconut milk, fragrant lemongrass and spices make this roast chicken an extra-special feast.

1 medium chicken (about 1.6 kg/3 lb 8 oz)
vegetable oil, for greasing and drizzling

FOR THE MARINADE

100 g (3½ oz) shallots, roughly chopped
2 lemongrass stalks, base only, finely chopped
1 large (25 g/1 oz) fresh red chilli
1 tsp ground turmeric
½ tsp ground white pepper
½ tsp ground coriander
200 ml (7 fl oz/generous ¾ cup) coconut milk
juice of ½ lime
2 big pinches of coarse sea salt

Blend all the ingredients for the marinade together in a blender until relatively smooth – flecks of chilli or lemongrass are ok.

Place the chicken in a greased roasting tin. Make a small slit at the bottom of the chicken breasts, then rub some of the spice marinade all over between the skin and flesh. Smear the rest of the marinade all over the chicken. Set aside for at least an hour – preferably overnight for maximum flavour.

When you're ready to cook, preheat the oven to 160°C/140°C fan/325°F/gas mark 3. If you left the chicken in the fridge overnight, let it come back up to room temperature first. Drizzle the chicken with a bit more oil, cover the tin with foil and place in the oven for 1 hour.

After an hour, remove the foil and let it roast, uncovered, for another hour, basting halfway through. Finally, whack the oven up to 220°C/200°C fan/425°F/gas mark 7 and roast for a further 30 minutes or so until the chicken's skin is golden brown and the juices run clear when the thigh is pierced with the tip of a sharp knife.

Remove the chicken from the oven and leave it to rest for at least 15 minutes before carving. It should be juicy and fall-apart tender. The pan juices will have all the wonderful flavours of turmeric, lemongrass and coconut, so make sure to spoon generously over the chicken to serve. Try this with Pandan Jasmine Rice (page 32) and a Cucumber Pineapple Salad (page 92); or you could just as happily eat this with roast potatoes.

SERVES 2–3 AS A SIDE

# Steamed Mussels with Coconut and Laksa Leaves

We need to eat more mussels. They are cheap, sustainable and so delicious. People get a bit intimidated by the idea of cooking mussels, but they're actually really quick and simple to prepare. In fact, it takes longer to eat a dish of mussels than it does to cook them. Once cleaned, you simply tip the mussels straight into a pot with aromatics and a splash of liquid, cover and let them steam. The mussels release their own sweet, salty juices to create an incredible broth with your ingredients – in this case, coconut, chilli and fragrant herbs.

500 g (1 lb 2 oz) fresh live mussels
1 tbsp vegetable oil or coconut oil
1 banana shallot, finely chopped
1 lemongrass stalk, base only, finely chopped
100 ml (3½ fl oz/scant ½ cup) coconut milk
1 bird's eye chilli, finely chopped
¼ tsp light brown sugar
zest and juice of ½ lime
pinch of fine sea salt, to taste
small handful of laksa leaves, finely chopped (see Note)

Clean the mussels by scrubbing them under cold running water to remove any barnacles or sand, then remove any visible beards by giving them a sharp pull. Discard any open mussels that do not close when tapped on the shell.

Heat the oil in a large heavy-based pot or wok. Over medium–high heat, fry the shallot and lemongrass until fragrant, about a couple of minutes.

Turn the heat up to high, tip in the mussels, coconut milk and chilli. Cover with a lid, and let cook for 3–4 minutes, or until all the mussels have opened up. Give the wok a good shake every now and then.

Stir in the sugar, lime zest and juice. Have a taste of the broth and season with salt if needed; the mussels will release their own salty juices, so you might not even need it. Remove any mussels that have not opened, then serve with a sprinkle of chopped laksa leaves.

Laksa leaves are also known as hot mint or Vietnamese coriander. As you may well have guessed, we sprinkle this fragrant herb over laksa in Singapore. If you can't get hold of it, a mix of fresh mint leaves and coriander will be delicious in this recipe.

SERVES 2–3 AS A SIDE

# Teochew Steamed Fish with Pickled Mustard Greens

Chinese cooks love serving whole steamed fish, because it really shows off the fresh flavour of the fish. In Teochew-style steamed fish, sour umami ingredients are used, such as brined plums, pickled mustard greens and/or tomatoes. This is traditionally done in a large steamer, but not many people own one large enough to fit a whole fish. Here, I often do it in the oven, especially with a larger fish. You wrap the fish in baking parchment with its seasonings, seal tightly so it steams instead of bakes, then unwrap the parcel at the table to oohs and aahs.

1 medium (300–400 g/10–14 oz) sea bass or sea bream, scaled and gutted
large pinch of coarse sea salt
¼ tsp white pepper
50 g (1¾ oz) pickled sour mustard greens (see Tip)
1 tbsp light soy sauce
1 tbsp Shallot Oil (page 209)
1 red bird's eye chilli, finely chopped
about 3 tbsp Shaoxing rice wine or water
thumb-sized piece (15 g/½ oz) fresh ginger, peeled and sliced into thin matchsticks
1 tbsp Fried Shallots (page 209)
200 g (7 oz) cherry tomatoes
small handful of coriander (cilantro), roughly chopped

Rub the fish all over with the salt and pepper, including inside its belly, and set aside. Soak the pickled mustard greens in a bowl of water for 10 minutes to remove some of their saltiness, then drain and slice thinly. Stir together the soy sauce, shallot oil and bird's eye chilli, with a splash of rice wine or water.

Preheat the oven to 180°C/160°C fan/350°F/gas mark 4. Cut a piece of baking parchment (parchment paper) large enough to wrap the fish with, and lay half of the sheet over a baking tray (pan). Pour the sauce over the fish. Scatter the mustard greens, ginger and fried shallots over the fish and tuck the cherry tomatoes around it. Now, wrap the other half of the sheet over the fish to form a packet, leaving a bit of space for the cooking juices, and seal tightly by folding and twisting the edges of the paper together. Place in the oven and cook for 20–25 minutes, depending on size.

Alternatively, if you have an XL steamer basket or a wok with a wire rack and lid, you can combine the ingredients in a shallow steamproof dish, cover and steam over high heat for 12–15 minutes. It's ready when the flesh at the thickest part is opaque and lifts off the bones effortlessly, and the cherry tomatoes are beginning to burst.

To serve, transfer the packet carefully to a serving platter. Unwrap at the table and finish with a sprinkle of chopped coriander leaves.

TIP

Pickled sour mustard greens can be found in vacuum sealed bags at most Asian shops, but if you can't get hold of them, plain sauerkraut makes a good supermarket substitute.

SERVES 2–3 AS A SIDE

# Drunken La La with Rice Wine

La la, or clams, is one of those dishes that's not just a joy to make; it's a noisy, clattering joy to eat. The clams taste of the sea – salty, briny and sweet – so you don't really have to do much else to make the dish taste good. Across cultures, cooks have combined clams with wine. This take on the classic combination makes use of Shaoxing rice wine, ginger and sesame oil for a wonderful, heady fragrance.

500 g (1 lb 2 oz) fresh live clams
1 tbsp vegetable oil
thumb-sized piece (15 g/½ oz) ginger, peeled and thinly sliced
2 garlic cloves, thinly sliced
1 red bird's eye chilli, chopped
100 ml (3½ fl oz/scant ½ cup) Shaoxing rice wine
2 tsp oyster sauce
1 tsp sesame oil
2 spring onions (scallions), thinly sliced diagonally

Rinse the clams well under cold running water. Chuck any with cracked shells and those that don't close when tapped sharply. Place the rest in a large basin of cold water and leave to stand for 30 minutes. The clams will spit out any sand that might be present inside the shells.

Heat the oil in a wok set over medium–high heat. Add the ginger to fry, stirring for a few seconds, before adding the garlic and chilli to fry for another 30 seconds or so.

Turn the heat up to high, and tip the drained clams, rice wine, oyster sauce and sesame oil into the wok. Stir-fry for another minute until they are all coated with the sauce.

Cover and cook on medium heat until the clams have opened and released their juices. This will depend on the size and type of your clams, but should only take minutes. Remove any clams that have not opened. Stir the spring onions through and serve.

SERVES 2–3 AS A SIDE

# Lime-Cured Fish with Chilli Padi and Pink Onions

This is one of my best-loved dinner party creations. It looks and tastes like it's way harder work to make than it actually is. Much like Peruvian ceviche, fresh fish is cured in citrus juices. Here, we use lime juice, as well as fish sauce for saltiness and bird's eye chilli for heat. The zippy acidic marinade lightly 'cooks' the raw fish and red onions, taking away their sharp edge. While the dish works beautifully as a simple side dish to have alongside other bits, I also like serving it as a starter or a snack with prawn crackers.

juice of 2 limes (about 4 tbsp)
2 tsp fish sauce
1½ tsp sugar, or to taste
1 bird's eye chilli, chopped
1 small red onion, thinly sliced
200 g (7 oz) skinless white fish fillets, such as sea bream or sea bass
small handful of coriander (cilantro), finely chopped

TO SERVE (OPTIONAL)
prawn crackers

To make the marinade, combine the lime juice, fish sauce, sugar and chilli, stirring well to dissolve the sugar. Taste and adjust seasoning to your liking; you might find you need a pinch more sugar if you have a particularly salty fish sauce.

Add the sliced red onions to the marinade and set aside for 15 minutes. The acidic juices will help to take away the onion's raw taste and lightly pickle them, mellowing both their flavour and colour.

Meanwhile, slice the fish fillets against the grain, at an angle, into ½ cm (¼ in) thin slices. Pour the marinade over the fish. The longer you leave it, the more 'cooked' the fish gets; I like to leave it for just 5 minutes.

To serve, arrange the fish and pink onions on a plate, dress with the citrusy milky marinade and sprinkle with the chopped coriander. To eat, get everyone to spoon a bit of everything onto a prawn cracker and shove the whole thing into their mouths.

SERVES 2–3 AS A SIDE

# Steamed Aubergines with Cherry Tomato Sambal

When steamed, aubergines (eggplants) become silky soft and almost creamy inside – a perfect sponge for soaking up any sauce. Here, I've topped the aubergine with a summery sambal, made with fresh cherry tomatoes. It brings together two of my favourite sauces to eat with aubergine: sambal chilli (a must-have at any Malay nasi padang stall) and tomato sauce (well-loved in all sorts of Italian classics like aubergine parmigiana). As the tomatoes fry, their sugars caramelise and give the sambal a rich, sweet–sour depth. This is a dish that really sings of hot sunny days – whether in sweltering Singapore or in a British back garden in August.

1 medium aubergine (eggplant) (about 250 g/9 oz)
2 tsp white rice vinegar, or white wine vinegar
2 tsp light soy sauce
small handful of Thai basil
small handful of fresh coriander (cilantro), finely chopped

FOR THE TOMATO SAMBAL TOPPING (SEE TIP)

50 g (1¾ oz) large red chillies, roughly chopped
2 garlic cloves
1 banana shallot, roughly chopped
100 g (3½ oz) cherry tomatoes, half roughly chopped
3 tbsp vegetable oil
juice of ½ lime (about 1 tbsp)
½ tsp light brown sugar
¼ tsp fine sea salt, or to taste

Slice the aubergine into 2 cm (¾ in) thick, finger-length batons. Now, place the aubergine batons in a large bowl of water with the vinegar, and leave for 10 minutes. This extra step helps the aubergine keep its beautiful purple/white colours.

To make the tomato sambal topping, pound the chillies, garlic, shallot and half the cherry tomatoes using a pestle and mortar or whizz in a small blender until you get a coarse paste. Heat the oil in a wok or large frying pan set over medium heat and fry the sambal for 15 minutes, until fragrant and the oil seeps back out. Quarter the remaining cherry tomatoes and add to the pan, frying until their skins blister and burst. Lightly crush some of the tomatoes so they release their juices into the sambal. Stir in the lime juice, sugar and salt.

While the sambal is frying, steam the aubergines. Stack them in a steamer basket, and set over gently boiling water. Cover and steam over high heat for 8–10 minutes until they're soft but still firm enough to hold their shape. Transfer the steamed aubergines to your serving plate, arranging them in a line down the plate and drizzle the light soy sauce over evenly.

Warm up the cherry tomato sambal again so it's sizzling, then spoon it over the aubergines. Make sure you get everything in the pan, including the bright red chilli-spiked oil. Sprinkle the Thai basil and coriander over to serve.

If you've got my essential Sambal Tumis (page 204) already sitting in the fridge, you can shortcut this: gently fry the cherry tomatoes in oil until they burst, then stir in 2 tablespoons of Sambal Tumis and a pinch of salt.

SERVES 3–4 AS A SIDE

# Kam Heong Fried Cauliflower

There's no sauce that better shows off the unique makeup of Singapore. *Kam heong* (or 'golden and fragrant' in Cantonese) sauce was created by the ever-ingenious *tze char* chefs, bringing together ingredients from almost every culture: curry powder, soy sauces, bird's eye chillies and curry leaves. This sauce tastes good with everything, from fried chicken to seafood. I've created a vegan-friendly dish here using cauliflower, as you really won't miss the meat in this recipe.

150 g (5½ oz/1¼ cups) plain (all-purpose) flour
4 tbsp cornflour (cornstarch)
1 tsp baking powder
¼ tsp ground turmeric
¼ tsp fine sea salt
300 ml (10 fl oz/1¼ cups) cold sparkling or soda water
1 small head of cauliflower (500 g/1 lb 2 oz), broken into bite-sized florets
vegetable oil, for frying
1 banana shallot, finely chopped
10 fresh or frozen curry leaves
1 red bird's eye chilli, finely chopped

FOR THE SAUCE

1 tbsp curry powder (see Note)
1 tbsp taucheo
2 tsp dark soy sauce
2 tsp light soy sauce
1 tsp light brown sugar
100 ml (3½ fl oz/scant ½ cup) water

Whisk together the flour, cornflour (cornstarch), baking powder, turmeric and salt in a large bowl. Make a well in the middle and slowly pour in the sparkling or soda water, whisking to form a smooth batter. Add the cauliflower florets and toss through to coat.

Heat 1 cm (½ in) of oil in a wide frying pan over medium–high heat. To know when the oil is ready, stick a pair of wooden chopsticks into the hot oil – it should sizzle instantly with tiny bubbles. Gently drop the cauliflower into the hot oil, first shaking off any excess batter. Shallow-fry for 5 minutes or until golden, flipping halfway. Remove with a slotted spoon and drain on kitchen paper (paper towels) while you finish up the rest.

After the cauliflower florets are all fried, stir to combine the ingredients for the sauce. Leave a couple of tablespoons of oil in the pan. Add the chopped shallots, curry leaves and chilli and fry until very fragrant. Pour in the sauce. Once bubbling, return the fried cauliflower to the pan and toss through to coat. Serve immediately.

Any store-bought curry powder will work here, but to make up a very simple one out of some basic spices, use 1½ teaspoon ground coriander, 1 teaspoon ground turmeric, 1 teaspoon ground cumin, ½ teaspoon chilli powder (Kashmiri or mild) and a generous dash of black pepper.

# ONE-DIS

## CHAPTER SIX

# MEALS

## CHAPTER SIX

# SIX

Many Singaporean hawker classics are perfect one-dish meals. It makes sense as most hawker centre stalls are geared for serving a customer at once. At home, I like making meals like this when I want to curl up on the sofa and hug a bowl of something comforting.

Some of these dishes come together in one pan or wok. Ingredients are thrown together in the cooking process, where their colours, flavours and textures meet and marry. The rice in a clay pot absorbs the flavour of Chinese sausage and shiitake mushrooms as they cook together. The heat from a smoking wok brings rice, eggs and sambal together to create something spicier and sexier than the sum of its parts – *nasi goreng*.

The other dishes come together on one plate or bowl. Various elements are cooked or prepared separately, but it's when they are combined in the final stages that the dish really sings. Delicate, juicy wonton dumplings are great, but tossed with chewy egg noodles and a sweet soy and ketchup sauce, they are made infinitely better.

Rice vermicelli, tofu puffs and prawns are all tasty things but unremarkable on their own. Pour a rich, heady laksa broth over, finish with fresh peppery herbs and suddenly, everything comes to life.

This chapter is all about dishes that are a complete package by themselves. Here, sides are not necessary (though they are always welcome).

SERVES 2–3

# Hainanese Chicken Rice

This is a dish brought over by the Hainanese immigrants and looks deceptively plain: poached chicken, served with rice cooked in the chicken broth and fat. But done right, it's a masterful lesson in drawing flavours out of basic ingredients and carrying them through all the elements on a plate. The Singaporean twist to the original Hainan dish is the addition of pandan leaves or lemongrass for extra fragrance, as well as a punchy chilli sauce. This used to be a dish I would reserve for weekends, as the traditional method of poaching a whole chicken requires a fair bit more time – and more friends to feed! Using chicken thighs means I can do this in half the time, with all the flavour for a midweek treat. Get the best chicken you can afford – corn-fed/free-range/organic – as it's such a simple dish, you want your few key ingredients to really shine.

4 chicken thighs (about 600 g/1 lb 5 oz), skin on and bone in
coarse sea salt, for rubbing
about 750 ml (1¼ pints/ 3 cups) water
1 garlic bulb, smashed
2 thumb-sized pieces (30 g/1 oz) of fresh ginger, peeled and smashed
2 pandan leaves, knotted, or 2 lemongrass stalks, lightly bashed
2 spring onions (scallions), chopped
150 g (5½ oz/¾ cup) jasmine rice, rinsed and drained
2 tbsp light soy sauce
¼ tsp fine sea salt, or to taste
2 tsp sesame oil

FOR THE GINGER-GARLIC SAUCE

1 tbsp grated ginger
1 tbsp grated garlic
½ tsp light brown sugar
¼ tsp fine sea salt, or to taste
1 tbsp vegetable oil
1 tsp sesame oil
1 tbsp chicken stock from poaching chicken

TO SERVE

Ginger-garlic Sauce (above)
Garlic Chilli Sauce (page 206)
thick dark soy sauce or kecap manis
chicken stock from poaching chicken
ground white pepper, to taste
½ cucumber, sliced
small handful of fresh coriander (cilantro)

Prepare the chicken by trimming any visible fat – set it aside for later. Rub the chicken all over with generous pinches of coarse sea salt. Place the chicken in a large pot, wide enough to fit the thighs in a single layer. Pour in just enough of the water to submerge the chicken, but you might need a bit more or less depending on the size of your pot. Add half the garlic, ginger, pandan or lemongrass and spring onions to the pot and bring to a rolling boil then turn the heat down to a bare simmer. Cook for 10 minutes, skimming off any scum. Turn the heat off and let the chicken sit in the hot water, covered, for another 15 minutes.

Meanwhile, render the chicken fat by cooking over moderate heat in a pan. Discard the solids. Once the chicken is cooked, remove and place straight into a large bowl of iced water. This will give it a nice springy texture. You also now have a pot of flavourful stock from poaching the chicken!

Combine the rice with 250 ml (8 fl oz/1 cup) of chicken stock, the rendered chicken fat, sesame oil, the remaining ginger, garlic, pandan and spring onion. Season with the fine sea salt. Cook in the rice cooker or on the stovetop following the instructions on page 30, before fluffing and serving.

While the rice is cooking, get all the other bits ready to serve. Make the ginger-garlic sauce by combining the ginger, garlic, sugar and salt in a small heatproof bowl. Heat the oils in a small pan and pour over the mixture, then stir in the chicken stock. De-bone and slice the chicken, then drizzle with the remaining teaspoon of sesame oil and soy sauce. Get your other dipping sauces ready in little saucers. Warm up the chicken broth and season with salt and white pepper, to taste.

To serve, arrange the cut chicken and cucumbers over the warm rice, alongside your various sauces and little bowls of chicken broth. Garnish with the fresh coriander.

PAGE 136

SERVES 4

# Katong Curry Laksa

This spicy coconut-laced noodle soup is perhaps one of the region's most well-loved culinary exports. To create that heavenly broth, we start with a *rempah* made from lemongrass, dried shrimp and spices, then stir in coconut milk and stock. The laksa I grew up with uses prawn stock, made simply by simmering leftover prawn heads and shells to deliver a deep umami punch from the sea. Another special element of a Singaporean laksa, particularly along a stretch of road in the Katong area, is that the noodles are cut into short strands, so you can conveniently slurp it with just a soup spoon. In fact, the most famous laksa stalls often charge extra for chopsticks!

12 large (400 g/14 oz) king prawns (shrimp), shell-on
1 litre (1¾ pints/4 cups) water
1½ tsp fine sea salt, or to taste
2 tsp light brown sugar, or to taste
4 tbsp vegetable oil
200 ml (7 fl oz/generous ¾ cup) coconut milk
8 tofu puffs, halved
200 g (7 oz) dried thick rice vermicelli noodles (1.6 mm) (see Tip)
2 hard-boiled eggs, peeled and halved
100 g (3½ oz) beansprouts
small handful of laksa leaves, very finely sliced (or a mix of mint and coriander/cilantro)
Sambal Tumis (page 204) or Sambal Belacan (page 205), to serve (optional)

FOR THE REMPAH (SPICE PASTE)

5 dried red Kashmiri chillies, soaked in hot water until softened
2 tbsp dried shrimps, soaked in enough hot water to cover until softened
100 g (3½ oz) shallots, roughly chopped
2 lemongrass stalks, base only, finely chopped
thumb-sized piece (15 g/½ oz) fresh ginger, peeled and roughly chopped
2 tsp ground turmeric
2 tsp ground coriander
½ tsp ground white pepper

We'll start by making our prawn stock. Bring the water to the boil in a pan and season with the salt and sugar. Add the prawns, turn the heat down to medium, and cook until the prawns just turn orange. Fish out the prawns and remove their heads and shells, leaving their tails on for aesthetics. Set the peeled cooked prawns aside and return the shells and heads to the pot to simmer for another 30 minutes, before straining.

Meanwhile, we'll get our rempah going. Drain the chillies and dried shrimp, reserving the shrimp soaking liquid. Pound all the spice paste ingredients using a pestle and mortar or whizz in a small blender until you get a fine paste. If blending, you might need to add a tiny splash of water to help the paste come together. Heat the oil in a large pot set over medium heat. When hot, add the spice paste, turn the heat down to low and fry for 15 minutes, or until the oil seeps back out.

We can now bring the laksa broth together. To the pot of fried rempah, add the coconut milk, strained prawn stock and dried shrimp soaking liquid. Stir and bring to a gentle boil, then add the tofu puffs. Cook for a couple of minutes before turning the heat off. Taste the laksa broth at this point and adjust with more salt or sugar if needed.

Now it's assembly time. Cook the rice noodles in plenty of boiling water until cooked, about 3–5 minutes depending on packet instructions. Drain and rinse with cold water to stop them clumping, then snip into shorter strands with kitchen scissors. Divide the noodles into bowls, and top with the cooked prawns, eggs and beansprouts. Make sure the laksa broth is still piping hot – if not warm it up again, taking care not to let it come to a rolling boil. Pour the hot laksa broth and tofu puffs over, making sure to submerge the noodles. Finish with a sprinkle of laksa leaves and a dollop of sambal.

For traditional Singapore laksa, and for the best slurping experience, thick rice vermicelli is preferred. They are spaghetti-like in shape but made of rice instead of wheat. But if you can't get hold of them, feel free to replace them with thin rice vermicelli, available in most supermarkets. They don't need boiling – just pour hot boiling water over, cover and soak for 5 minutes until soft, before draining.

SERVES 2–3

# Uncle's 'Dry' Laksa

When most people think of laksa, a bowl of brothy slurpy noodles comes first to mind, so a dry laksa might sound like a curious thing. I first had dry laksa at a friend's place. Her father would politely interrupt every maths revision session with a plate of food, because 'you can't study on an empty stomach'. I vividly remember Uncle's dry laksa; he had tried it at a trendy new café and recreated it for us, using store-bought laksa paste, fresh rice noodles, king prawns and herbs. It had everything I loved about a curry laksa, but this was significantly less messy to eat over a pile of textbooks. It most definitely helped us pass our exams! Here, I've used the laksa *rempah* from page 137 and fresh egg noodles, readily available at most supermarkets.

180 g (6 oz) raw jumbo king prawns (shrimps), peeled, tails on
½ quantity of Laksa Spice Paste (page 137)
pinch of coarse sea salt
3 tbsp vegetable oil
100 ml (3½ fl oz/scant ½ cup) coconut milk
1 tbsp fish sauce
1 tsp light brown sugar
400 g (14 oz) pack of fresh egg noodles
100 g (3½ oz) beansprouts
1 lime, juice of ½, the remaining ½ sliced into wedges to serve
handful of laksa leaves (or Thai basil, basil or mint leaves)
handful of coriander (cilantro), roughly torn
Sambal Tumis (page 204) or Sambal Belacan (page 205), to serve (optional)

To devein the prawns, cut down the back of each from the head to just before the tail, lift out the black line and pull to remove. This also helps the prawn to curl up into a pretty butterfly shape later. Toss with 1 tablespoon of the laksa paste and a pinch of salt.

Set a wok or large frying pan over a high heat and add half the oil. Once smoking hot, add the prawns in a single layer. Fry until they turn orange and char on the edges. Remove and set aside.

Add the remaining oil and laksa paste to the wok and turn the heat down to low. Fry for 10 minutes, stirring often, until very fragrant. Add the coconut milk, fish sauce and sugar and stir until most of the liquid cooks off – the sauce will darken and you will see the coconut oil separating from the sauce.

Now whack the heat back up and add the noodles, mixing and tossing to make sure they're well coated with the sauce. Finally, return the prawns to the wok, along with the beansprouts and lime juice. Give it another few tosses until everything is heated through and integrated. Taste at this point, adding a pinch more salt or fish sauce if you think it needs it.

Turn the heat off and stir in the herbs. Dish onto plates and serve with the lime wedges and sambal.

All spice pastes can be used to add an instant pop of flavour to stir-fries, so take this recipe as a little guide or inspiration to create new special dishes or stretch leftovers.

SERVES 2 GENEROUSLY, OR UP TO 3

# Chilli Crab Spaghetti

Chilli crab is one of the most iconic dishes of Singapore. The original dish consists of whole mud crabs, stir-fried in a sweet, spicy and savoury tomato sauce, then served with deep-fried *mantou* (Chinese steamed buns) and bowls of lemon water – the latter to wash your sauce-drenched hands with. But as with all the best foods in Singapore, this dish has continued to evolve, beyond its first invention back in the 1950s. Young Singaporean chefs have turned this explosive dish into a pasta sauce, and you'll find chilli crab spaghetti served in many modern bistros. Here is my version, using cooked crab meat for ease. I use both white and brown meat; the latter adds a rich seafood depth to the sauce, akin to shrimp paste.

4 tbsp olive oil
200 g (7 oz) dried spaghetti
½ tsp fine sea salt, plus more for boiling pasta
½ x 400 g (14 oz) tin finely chopped tomatoes
2 tsp taucheo
1 tsp light brown sugar
100 g (3½ oz) brown crab meat
100 g (3½ oz) white crab meat
small handful of fresh coriander (cilantro), finely chopped

FOR THE REMPAH (SPICE PASTE)

1 banana shallot, roughly chopped
2 garlic cloves
thumb-sized (15 g/½ oz) piece fresh ginger, peeled and roughly chopped
1 large red chilli, roughly chopped
1 lemongrass stalk, roughly chopped
1 tsp tomato ketchup

Pound all the spice paste ingredients using a pestle and mortar or whizz in a small blender until you get a fine paste. If using a blender, you might need to add 1–2 tablespoons of water. Heat the olive oil in a large frying pan set over medium heat and fry the paste for 10 minutes until fragrant and the oil seeps back out.

Boil the spaghetti in a pot of well-salted water according to the packet instructions until al dente – tender, but resistant to the bite.

Meanwhile, to the spice paste, add the tinned tomatoes, taucheo, sugar and ½ teaspoon of salt and bring to a simmer. Cook uncovered for 5 minutes, stirring occasionally, until it thickens. Add the brown crab meat and stir to mix through. Now turn the heat off and fold the white crab meat into the sauce.

The spaghetti should be done by now so drain, reserving some of the pasta water. Tip the spaghetti into the pan of chilli crab sauce and toss through to make sure the strands are all well coated, adding a splash of pasta water to loosen if needed. Divide into warm bowls and finish with the fresh coriander.

SERVES 2

# Nasi Goreng

You will find fried rice in almost every rice-eating nation, and Singapore is no exception. Given our cultural diversity, there are countless varieties of fried rice, but the one I always turn to is this Malay-style fried rice, seasoned with kecap manis and sambal. It's a good recipe to have in your back pocket, as you can turn leftover rice and the bits and bobs sitting around in your crisper drawer into something truly special. I've used green beans here, but you could just as easily use the same volume of any crisp green vegetables, odd ends of carrots or celery, or even frozen peas. The only thing I would highly encourage you to keep are the runny fried eggs, as when broken, the yolks spill into the fried rice, adding richness to each spoonful.

3 tbsp vegetable oil
2 large free-range eggs
pinch of fine sea salt, to taste
1 banana shallot, finely chopped
100 g (3½ oz) green beans, chopped into 1 cm (½ in) lengths
2 rice bowls (300 g/10½ oz/ 2½ cups) cooked long-grain rice (see Tip)
1½ tbsp light soy sauce
1 tbsp kecap manis
1 red chilli, sliced
1 tbsp Sambal Tumis, plus more to serve (page 204)
juice of ½ lime

TO SERVE

few sprigs of fresh coriander (cilantro), roughly torn
Fried Shallots (page 142)
½ cucumber, sliced
handful of prawn crackers (optional)

Heat the oil in a wok set over medium–high heat. Carefully crack the eggs into the hot oil and season with a pinch of salt. Fry until the whites set and turn golden brown on the edges – you might want to spoon the hot oil over the whites to help them set. Remove with a slotted spatula and set aside, keeping them warm.

Add the shallots to the remaining oil in the wok and stir-fry until fragrant and light golden. Then add the green beans to cook, frying until they are bright green and tender. Now, whack the heat up so the oil is smoking hot, before adding the cold cooked rice. Spread out the rice and jab lightly with your spatula to break up any lumps. Stir in the soy sauce, kecap manis, chilli and sambal tumis, stirring and tossing to make sure all the rice grains are well coated. Keep stir-frying until the seasonings evaporate and the rice is heated through. When you see the edges of the rice start to caramelise, squeeze the lime over and give it a final stir through.

Divide the nasi goreng onto two plates and top with a fried egg each. Finish with a sprinkle of coriander, fried shallots and an extra dollop of sambal. I also like to arrange a few cucumber slices and prawn crackers alongside the rice – they add a delightful crunchy textural contrast to the dish.

The best fried rice uses day-old rice from the fridge, because the grains are drier – use your hands to break the rice up into smaller lumps before adding to the wok. If using freshly cooked rice, to prevent clumping, spread the rice out on a tray for 10 minutes first to allow the steam to evaporate.

# Childhood Wonton Mee

**SERVES 2**

This is a noodle dish you'll find in many countries with a large Cantonese community – Hong Kong, of course, as well as Thailand, Malaysia and Singapore. It's no wonder this dish is so popular – springy egg noodles and slippery, juicy wonton dumplings are a match made in heaven. They can be served 'wet' in a light chicken broth, or 'dry' tossed in a light soy dressing. Singapore has its own spin on the classic dish; we like things sweeter, so the noodles are dressed in a sweet dark soy sauce and sambal (for the grownups), or ketchup (for the children). What marked my transition from childhood to adulthood was the gradual addition of sambal to my wonton mee. In the recipe below, you've got a choice of either, or feel free to mix the two to a ratio of your liking.

100 g (3½ oz) greens, such as Chinese broccoli or Tenderstem broccoli
10 homemade wonton dumplings (page 146)
2 nests of thin egg noodles (200 g/7 oz fresh or 125 g/4½ oz dried)
1 tbsp Fried Shallots (page 209)
1 spring onion (scallion), finely chopped
1 tbsp Pickled Green Chillies (page 208) (optional)

### FOR THE NOODLE DRESSING

2 tbsp dark soy sauce
1 tbsp kecap manis
1 tbsp Shallot Oil (page 209)
1 tbsp tomato ketchup, or Sambal Tumis (page 204)

Put two saucepans of water on the stove to boil. Stir together the ingredients for the dressing and divide among two bowls.

In one saucepan of water, blanch the greens until they are tender.

In the other saucepan, lower the wontons carefully into the boiling water. Turn the heat down so it is at an aggressive simmer. When the dumplings float to the top, let cook for another minute or so then remove with a slotted spoon.

When the greens are done, remove and set aside. In that same pot of water, boil the noodles until they are just cooked. Fresh noodles only take seconds while dried noodles will take about 2 minutes – steal a little strand to test. Drain with a sieve (fine mesh strainer), rinse in cold water, then dip again in hot water to warm up just before slipping into the bowls of sauces. This process gives the noodles a wonderful springy bite. Toss with a pair of chopsticks so each strand is well-coated with the sauce.

Place the wontons on the side of the noodles, along with the blanched greens from earlier. Finish with the fried shallots, chopped spring onion and pickled green chillies – the latter is optional but makes a classic sharp accompaniment to the sweet, salty noodles.

MAKES 40

# Two Easy Homemade Wontons

Here's a little guide to making and folding your own wontons. Once you've mastered that, you can play around with fillings. I've shared two filling recipes to start you off. The first is pork and prawn – a classic you will recognise in most Chinese restaurants. It's a classic for a reason, because it's wonderfully savoury and juicy, and the prawns give sweetness and a tantalising hint of orange colour through the translucent dumpling skins when cooked.

The second is a vegetarian filling I developed for Low Carbon Chinatown, a community project by my friend Ling to create more environmentally conscious versions of Londoners' favourite Chinese dishes. I use tofu as it's a brilliant flavour sponge; carrot, to mimic the sweetness and colour of prawns; and finally, leek stir-fried until savoury and sticky to bind everything together.

1 pack of fresh or frozen wonton wrappers

FOR THE CLASSIC PORK AND PRAWN FILLING

200 g (7 oz) fatty minced (ground) pork
100 g (3½ oz) raw peeled prawns (shrimp), finely chopped
2 spring onions (scallions), finely chopped
1 tsp grated fresh ginger
1½ tbsp light soy sauce
1 tsp Shaoxing rice wine
½ tsp sesame oil
¼ tsp white pepper
¼ tsp fine sea salt
2–3 tbsp cold water

FOR THE TOFU, FRIED LEEK AND CARROT FILLING

200 g (7 oz) extra-firm tofu
1 leek, thinly sliced
1 tbsp vegetable oil
3 tbsp light soy sauce
1 large carrot, grated
1 tsp grated fresh ginger
2 tsp sesame oil
¼ tsp white pepper

**How to make the filling**

FOR THE CLASSIC PORK AND PRAWN FILLING

In a large mixing bowl, combine all the ingredients. Stir in the water as you go, making sure the meat fully absorbs the liquid and turns into a sticky paste. 'Beating' water in is key to a nice juicy wonton.

FOR THE TOFU, FRIED LEEK AND CARROT FILLING

Drain the tofu and finely chop until you get a mince-like consistency. In a hot frying pan, fry the leek in oil until softened, about 5 minutes. Add 1 tablespoon of the soy sauce and cook for another minute until most of the soy sauce disappears. The leek should smell really fragrant, reduce in volume and also become a bit sticky, helping you bring the filling together. Bring the fried leek, tofu and rest of the ingredients together in a large mixing bowl, stirring until well combined.

**How to fold**

If using fresh wrappers, make sure they're kept under a damp cloth while you're folding, or they will dry out and tear easily. If using frozen wrappers, make sure to defrost in the fridge overnight until soft and pliable; you can't speed it up by defrosting on the counter or the wrappers turn into a soggy mess.

Get your station ready: your bowl of filling, a small bowl of water, a tray to lay out your finished dumplings.

To fold, dip your finger in the water and wet the edge of a wonton wrapper. Place a tablespoon of filling in the middle. Fold in half to get a rectangle, making sure to press around the filling to remove any air pockets. Wet the bottom corners and bring together, towards you, pressing to seal. Or, for the lazy, just bring all the corners together, scrunch up and press to seal.

**How to freeze**

At this stage, you could freeze the uncooked wonton dumplings, in a single layer, on a tray lined with baking parchment (parchment paper). Once frozen, pop them into a freezer bag for easy meals. They cook brilliantly straight from frozen.

**How to cook**

Bring a saucepan of water to the boil and lower the wonton dumplings carefully into the boiling water. Turn the heat down so it is at an aggressive simmer. When the wontons float to the top, cook for another minute or so, before removing with a slotted spoon. Serve either with noodles (page 144); or in chicken or vegetable stock, seasoned to taste with salt, white pepper and sesame oil.

SERVES 2

# Char Bee Hoon with Wild Garlic and Fried Tofu

Ironically, I had never heard of 'Singapore Noodles' until I left Singapore. Fried rice vermicelli is best known as *char bee hoon* by many Singaporean Chinese families, a crowd-pleasing dish that's most often eaten at home or packed into extra-large foil trays for potlucks. It's a versatile stir-fry that goes well with all sorts of ingredients (usually what's left over in the fridge), but there will almost always be these obligatory standbys: savoury shiitake mushrooms and pungent alliums, such as Chinese garlic chives. Here I've used British wild garlic, an edible joy of spring that grows free and in abundance in damp woodlands. I've also added tofu, fried first until golden and pillowy. I wrote this with a vegan friend in mind, but this is one dish that will please the vegans and non-vegans alike.

100 g (3½ oz) dried thin rice vermicelli noodles (0.5 mm)
4 dried shiitake mushrooms
1 tbsp vegetarian mushroom 'oyster' sauce
½ tsp light brown sugar
200 g (7 oz) firm tofu
vegetable oil, for frying
pinch of fine sea salt
1½ tbsp dark soy sauce
2 tsp toasted sesame oil, plus extra
½ tsp white pepper
2 shallots, chopped
large handful of wild garlic leaves (see Tip)
100 g (3½ oz) beansprouts
Pickled Green Chillies (page 208), to serve

Let's start with all the soaking. Soak the noodles in cold water until soft and pliable. Rinse and soak the dried mushrooms in just enough hot water to cover, about 200 ml (7 fl oz/generous ¾ cup), along with the 'oyster' sauce and sugar. This is a top tip from my mum: as the mushrooms don't get much time cooking in a saucy braise later, you want to make sure they marinate while they rehydrate and soak up flavour now.

In the meantime, drain and cut the tofu into three 2 cm (¾ in) pieces and pat dry. Heat ½ cm (¼ in) of oil in a large frying pan set over medium heat. Add the tofu in a single layer, sprinkle with a pinch of salt and fry until golden, flipping halfway through. Set aside on kitchen paper (paper towels) to drain.

The noodles should be soft and the mushrooms plump by now. Drain the noodles and set aside. Drain the mushrooms, making sure to squeeze any liquid back into the bowl. Destalk the mushrooms and slice thinly, reserving the soaking liquid. To the soaking liquid, stir in the dark soy sauce, sesame oil and white pepper – this will form our seasoned mushroom stock.

Set a wok or large frying pan over medium heat. Add 2 tablespoons of vegetable oil and when hot, add the chopped shallots to fry. Once they turn light golden and fragrant, add the mushrooms and stir-fry for another minute or so.

Add the fried tofu, along with half of the seasoned mushroom stock. Stir-fry for a minute, so the tofu absorbs flavour from the stock. Now, stir in the rest of the mushroom stock and bring everything to a bubbling simmer. Gently push the tofu to the side and add the drained noodles, making sure they're immersed in the stock. Using a pair (or even two pairs) of chopsticks, constantly jiggle and toss the noodles so that each strand soaks up all of the delicious mushroom stock.

Once the noodles are no longer wet, add the wild garlic and beansprouts. If you find things sticking, drizzle in a bit more sesame oil. Keep tossing gently until they wilt and everything is well mixed through. Dish onto plates, making sure to get a bit of everything, and serve with pickled green chillies.

**TIP**

If you can't get hold of wild garlic, or if you have out-of-season *bee hoon* cravings, you can replace them with half a bunch of spring onions, cut into strips.

SERVES 2

# Mum's Steamed Pumpkin Rice

Pumpkin rice is strictly homestyle; I have never seen it served in restaurants or even at hawker stalls. While this dish looks unassuming and is made simply (straight inside a rice cooker), it tastes far from ordinary. As the rice steams, it takes on the pumpkin's sweetness, the dried shrimps' saltiness, the mushrooms' umami and the fried garlic's aroma. It was the perfect one-pot dish for my mum to feed four hungry children with after school. Today it remains a perfect one-pot dinner to make for myself, especially when it's squash season. While named 'pumpkin rice', any sweet, dense winter squash will do. Avoid the large orange ones you carve for Halloween and look instead for varieties such as the Delica pumpkin, kabocha squash or butternut squash.

3 tbsp dried shrimps
4 dried shiitake mushrooms
about 250 ml (8 fl oz/1 cup) hot water, for soaking
1 tbsp light soy sauce
1 tbsp dark soy sauce
150 g (5½ oz/¾ cup) jasmine rice, rinsed and drained
1 tsp toasted sesame oil
¼ tsp white pepper
2 tbsp vegetable oil
1 shallot, finely chopped
4 garlic cloves, finely chopped
300 g (10½ oz) pumpkin or sweet winter squash, peeled and chopped into 2 cm (¾ in) pieces
pinch of fine sea salt

TO FINISH

1 spring onion (scallion), finely chopped
Chilli Garlic Sauce (page 206) or Crispy Chilli Oil (page 210) (optional)

Soak the dried shrimps in just enough hot water to cover, about 3–4 tablespoons. Soak the shiitake mushrooms in the hot water, with the light soy sauce and ½ tablespoon of the dark soy sauce stirred in. When the shrimps soften and the mushrooms are plump, drain but reserve both soaking liquids – they are full of umami flavour and will form our stock for cooking the rice with later. Make sure to squeeze the mushrooms over the bowl so you don't lose any juices, before removing the stems and slicing thinly.

Place the washed jasmine rice in a rice cooker or a medium saucepan, along with the reserved mushroom and shrimp stock, sesame oil and white pepper.

Separately, heat the oil in a wok or frying pan set over medium heat. Add the shallot, garlic and dried shrimp and stir-fry until golden and fragrant. Then add the pumpkin, along with a pinch of salt, and fry for 5 more minutes. Stir in the remaining dark soy sauce and a tiny splash of water, about 3–4 tablespoons, to help deglaze any browned bits from the bottom of the pan. Now tip the fried pumpkin mixture over the rice.

Let the rice cooker do its magic or cook on the stovetop following the instructions on page 30. Once cooked, leave for 5 minutes before fluffing and serving. Finish with a sprinkle of chopped spring onions and a drizzle of chilli sauce or chilli oil if you like a bit of kick.

SERVES 2

# Clay Pot Rice with Shiitake and Chinese Sausage

This is one of my favourite fuss-free one-pot meals. Traditionally, the clay pot is set over a charcoal fire and you bring the finished dish straight to the table, lifting the lid to a smoky fragrance and oohs and aahs. Today, the reality is that most of us will be cooking this over a regular stove, so if you can't get hold of a clay pot, a small heavy-bottomed pot with a tight lid will do. The idea is that you want the rice to steam, absorbing the flavours from the Chinese sausage and mushrooms; and the bottom layer to char, forming a delicious crispy crust.

150 g (5½ oz/¾ cup) uncooked jasmine rice
small handful of dried shiitake mushrooms
250 ml (8 fl oz/1 cup) hot water, for soaking
1 tbsp light soy sauce
1 tsp oyster sauce
1 tbsp vegetable oil
1 tsp sesame oil
2 garlic cloves, finely sliced
1 Chinese sausage, sliced diagonally
small handful of greens, such as pak choi (bok choi), trimmed
1 tsp kecap manis
1 spring onion (scallion), finely chopped

This is a quick recipe but calls for a fair amount of (inactive) soaking time in advance. Soak the clay pot the night before – this prevents it cracking over the heat. Soak the rice in cold water for 30 minutes – this helps it cook more quickly and evenly in the clay pot. Soak the dried shiitake in the hot water, with the soy sauce and oyster sauce stirred in, for 30 minutes.

When the shiitake mushrooms are soft and plump, drain, squeezing the liquid out, and slice. Reserve the liquid – it's full of flavour and forms a mushroom stock for cooking our rice with.

Heat the clay pot over medium heat. Drizzle the vegetable oil and sesame oil down the sides. Add the garlic and fry until golden. Then add the drained, rinsed rice. Lightly sauté to coat the grains with oil.

Pour in the mushroom stock and bring to a simmer. Arrange the Chinese sausage and mushrooms over. Cover and turn the heat down to low and cook for 10 minutes. Uncover the pot and arrange your greens on top. Cover again and turn the heat up to high for 2 minutes.

Serve straight from the clay pot. In Singapore, we finish the dish with kecap manis, spring onions and more sesame oil. Dig in, making sure you get the crispy bits at the bottom – the bit we would all fight over.

TIP

Chinese sausage is a dried, cured sausage that can be found on the shelves of Asian supermarkets. If you can't get hold of it, you can use 200 g (7 oz) boneless, skinless chicken thigh pieces, marinated in 2 tablespoons of oyster sauce and 1 teaspoon of sesame oil.

# Hot Smoked Mackerel and Ginger Congee

SERVES 2

Congee is one of my ultimate comfort foods. The soft, warm rice porridge is just what I need to soothe myself when I'm not feeling great, whether physically or emotionally. I shared a recipe earlier in the book for plain congee (page 36) – rice simmered in water until the grains disintegrate, to be eaten with salty sides. The congee on this page needs no other accompaniments; it's a perfect hug in a bowl that's ready in no time at all. I start with leftover cooked rice (a constant in my fridge) to halve the cooking time. I also make use of smoked mackerel, ginger and spring onions to add an instant depth of flavour to the congee. The eggs are an extra bonus I've picked up from the congee hawkers – they're slipped straight into the hot congee and barely cooked, so the yolks are still runny. While light and soothing, each spoonful of congee yields something fun: salty smoked fish, creamy yolk, hot ginger and fresh spring onions.

1 rice bowl (150 g/5½ oz/¾ cup) cooked jasmine rice
500 ml (17 fl oz/2 cups) water or homemade stock (broth) (page 69)
½ tsp fine sea salt, or to taste
2 spring onions (scallion), finely chopped, white and green parts separated
thumb-sized piece (15 g/¼ oz) fresh ginger, peeled and sliced into thin matchsticks
2 smoked mackerel fillets
¼ tsp ground white pepper, plus more to serve
½ tsp sesame oil
2 free-range eggs
1–2 tsp light soy sauce
Fried Shallots (page 209) or Crispy Chilli Oil (page 210) (optional)

In a medium saucepan, bring the cooked rice and water or stock to the boil. If using water, add ½ teaspoon of salt. Once it comes up to the boil, add the white parts of the spring onions and most of the ginger, reserving the rest for a garnish. Cover, turn the heat to low and simmer for 20–30 minutes. Stir occasionally to loosen any grains that are sticking to the bottom, and top up with more water as necessary. You want to cook the rice until the grains soften and completely disintegrate into a porridge.

In the meantime, remove the skin from the smoked mackerel and flake into large pieces. Toss with the white pepper and sesame oil. Set half aside as garnish.

When the congee is almost ready, stir in half of the smoked mackerel and a couple of tablespoons of water to loosen the congee. Taste and season at this point – depending on the saltiness of your smoked mackerel or stock, you may not need to add any extra salt.

Now, crack the eggs into the saucepan, cover again and let the eggs poach gently in the hot congee until the whites are just set but the yolks are still runny.

To serve, scoop the congee into bowls, making sure each bowl has an egg, and top with the reserved smoked mackerel, ginger and green parts of the spring onions. Finish with an extra dash of white pepper, light soy sauce and fried shallots or chilli oil, to taste. In fact, the condiments are usually left on the counter or table, in little bottles/shakers, for diners to help themselves to.

SERVES 2

# Torn Noodles with Poached Egg and Watercress

One of my earliest memories of 'cooking' with my mother is making *mee hoon kueh* together. These are rustic handmade noodles, done without the fuss of a pasta machine. Flour and water are combined and kneaded into a simple dough, then roughly torn off and flattened between floury palms into crude squares (blobs, really, if you were to be honest about my sister and my handiwork). To stay true to the simplicity of the dish, I like to keep things as unfussy as possible: serve the cooked *mee hoon kueh* in hot broth, with an egg poached directly in the broth for ease. I also add marinated minced (ground) meat and watercress – they cook instantly and also help flavour the broth.

FOR THE NOODLES

150 g (5½ oz) plain (all-purpose) flour, plus extra for dusting
¼ tsp fine sea salt
100 ml (3½ fl oz/scant ½ cup) water
1 tbsp vegetable oil
1 tsp sesame oil

FOR THE MINCED MEAT

100 g (3½ oz) minced (ground) pork
1 tsp sesame oil
1 tsp oyster sauce
2 tsp light soy sauce
¼ tsp ground white pepper

TO ASSEMBLE

handful of watercress
500 ml (17 fl oz/2 cups) homemade chicken stock (page 69), or 1 stock cube dissolved in 500 ml (17 fl oz/2 cups) boiling water
2 free-range eggs
fine sea salt, to taste
2 tsp Shallot Oil (page 209) or Crispy Chilli Oil (page 210)
1 tbsp Fried Shallots (page 209)
1 spring onion (scallion), finely chopped

Add the flour to a large mixing bowl, making a little well in the middle. Dissolve the salt in water, then gradually add the salted water to the flour, stirring until it just comes together. You might not need all the water! Once you get a rough dough, add the vegetable oil and knead in the bowl for about 10 minutes, or until it becomes soft and bouncy. Cover and leave aside to rest for at least 1 hour.

Meanwhile, marinate the minced pork with the oil, sauces and pepper.

To form the noodles, tear bite-sized pieces from the dough, then stretch and flatten them between your palms. Place them on a lightly floured plate while you finish forming the rest. To cook the noodles, drop them straight into a pot of boiling water. The noodles are done when they float to the top. Drain, toss with the sesame oil and divide between two bowls. Arrange the watercress alongside the noodles.

In a separate pot, bring the stock to a gentle boil. Stir in the minced pork and let simmer until cooked. Crack and gently slip the eggs into the pot and leave until the whites are set and the yolks are still runny. Taste the broth at this point and season with salt; you might not even need it if you started with a seasoned stock, as the meat also has a salty marinade.

Ladle the hot broth, along with the poached eggs and pork into the bowls of noodles. The watercress will wilt instantly and lightly infuse the broth with its peppery leafy taste. Drizzle over your choice of flavoured oil, and top with the fried shallots and spring onions.

# CHAPTER SEVEN

# LITTLE

# BITES

## CHAPTER SEVEN

# SEVEN

Singaporeans love to eat and we find every window of opportunity to do so. Some of my favourite things to eat are the little bites that we tag onto or sneak in between 'real' meals – a cheeky second breakfast, a teatime tidbit or a midnight supper at the hawker centre with friends.

Unlike the run-of-the-mill processed and packaged snacks you buy from British corner shops, snacks in Singapore are fresh, varied and delightful.

You might find yourself tearing into chicken wings fried with spices or marinated with kecap manis then grilled until sticky – and licking your fingers after. Or you might chomp down on *kaya* toast – sweet pandan coconut jam and thick slabs of butter sandwiched between charred slices of bread and washed down with strong coffee. Or you might pop into your neighbourhood 7-Eleven store for mints and leave with a couple of tea-infused eggs. You might even, after a night out, be persuaded (easily) by your friends to order two dozen sticks of barbecued satay – smoky with the fragrance of charcoal and perfect for soaking up the drinks.

Whenever it is and whoever you're with, you can find space for a little bite and a reason to smile. I hope this chapter becomes an inspiration for you to make every little in-between moment in your day delicious.

TO MAKE ABOUT 24 MEATBALLS

# Five-Spice Ngoh Hiang Meatballs

Ngoh Hiang are traditionally quite labour-intensive things: five-spice-marinated minced (ground) pork, prawns and water chestnuts, carefully wrapped within paper-thin beancurd sheets and rolled into thin sausages, then deep-fried. My mum and auntie were known for their *ngoh hiang* and would spend whole days mixing, rolling and frying ahead of big family reunions. What I remember best are the bonus treats at the end of a day of *ngoh hiang* making – *ngoh hiang* meatballs. My mum would roll the leftover stuffing into crude balls and fry them until golden. We would devour these hot, fragrant meatballs as a snack, before the main event. Here in the UK, I skip the fiddly beancurd sheets and make them just like that.

500 g (1 lb 2 oz) fatty minced (ground) pork
180 g (6 oz) raw peeled prawns (shrimps), finely chopped
2 shallots, finely chopped
225 g (8 oz) tin (140 g/5 oz drained) of water chestnuts, finely chopped
1 tsp ground white pepper
1 tsp five-spice powder
3 tbsp light soy sauce
2 tbsp oyster sauce
3 tbsp cornflour (cornstarch)
1 large free-range egg, beaten
vegetable oil, for frying

TO SERVE

Sambal Belachan (page 205)
cucumber slices

In a large mixing bowl, combine all the ingredients for the meatballs, except the oil. This mixture is best mixed together with your hands, so roll your sleeves up! Use your fingers to knead and mix well. Once it comes together, use your hands to gather the mixture up with your hands and slap it back down into the bowl a few times, until it becomes sort of sticky and dense. This will help to give the meatballs a springier texture later. Now wet your hands and form the mixture into roughly 3 cm (1¼ in) large balls, using the palms of your hands to roll and smooth. Don't worry if they're not perfectly smooth as any rough edges just get extra crispy and brown later when you fry them!

To fry, heat about 3 cm (1¼ in) of oil in a wok set over medium–high heat. To check if the oil is ready, stick a pair of wooden chopsticks into the hot oil – it should sizzle instantly with tiny bubbles. Gently drop the meatballs into the oil one at a time. They should firm up in a few seconds, so you can even crowd them a bit without worrying about them sticking. Fry for about 5 minutes, gently stirring occasionally so they brown evenly. Remove with a slotted spoon and drain on kitchen paper (paper towels) while you finish up the rest. If you aren't a fan of deep-frying, you could also pan-fry them in a large frying pan – it will just take a bit more patience to flip and brown them on all sides evenly.

The meatballs are delicious served warm, on their own, but much better with a side of spicy sambal and cool, fresh cucumber slices.

MAKES 8–10 JUMBO-SIZED SATAY

# BBQ Chicken Satay with Tamarind Peanut Sauce

Growing up in 1990s Singapore, I have fond memories of the neighbourhood Satay Man and his mobile kitchen. You would know he was round the corner with the 'toot toot' of his motorcycle horn and the unmistakable whiff of smoke and spices. My sisters and I would then run out with plates and bowls for him to fill up with sticks of barbecued satay and that legendary peanut sauce. Traditionally, for the latter, you would use freshly roasted and ground peanuts, but I find a jar of good peanut butter – deep-roasted and crunchy – makes a brilliant everyday shortcut.

FOR THE REMPAH (SPICE PASTE)

100 g (3½ oz) shallots, roughly chopped
3 lemongrass stalks, base only, finely chopped (reserve the woody tops)
2 large fresh red chillies
1 tbsp ground coriander
1 tsp ground cumin
½ tsp ground turmeric
½ tsp fine sea salt
1½ tbsp light soy sauce
1½ tbsp light brown sugar
3 tbsp vegetable oil

FOR THE SATAY

300 g (10½ oz) boneless chicken thigh fillets, cut into 2.5 cm (1 in) pieces
10 bamboo skewers
vegetable oil, for grilling

FOR THE PEANUT SAUCE

3 tbsp vegetable oil
3 tbsp crunchy peanut butter
3 tbsp tamarind paste
about 150 ml (5½ fl oz/⅔ cup) water
fine sea salt, to taste

TO SERVE

1 cucumber, chopped into bite-sized chunks
½ red onion, sliced

I like to do all the prep work the night before, or at least 2 hours ahead. Pound all the spice paste ingredients using a pestle and mortar or whizz in a small blender until you get a fine paste. Mix half the spice paste with the chicken and set aside in the fridge. Soak the bamboo skewers in water, to prevent them from burning during cooking later. The next day, thread the chicken onto skewers, about 4–5 pieces per skewer.

To make the peanut sauce, fry the remaining spice paste in oil in a small frying pan set over medium heat until very fragrant, about 10 minutes. Stir often as there's sugar in this spice paste, and we want it to caramelise but not burn! Add the peanut butter and tamarind, frying for another few minutes until darkened. Stir in enough water to loosen, and bring to a simmer – the sauce should have a thick but pourable consistency. Taste and adjust the seasoning with a pinch more salt or sugar if needed, then set aside.

When ready to cook, fire up your barbecue; or in the likely event it is raining, set a cast-iron griddle pan over the stove on high heat. Grill the chicken for 6–8 minutes until golden brown and charred. You want to rotate the skewers every couple of minutes, brushing the chicken with oil while it cooks. Do as the Satay Man would and use the reserved lemongrass tops as a brush for extra fragrance. Bonus: it's no-waste!

Serve the satay straight away, with bowls of peanut sauce and chunks of cucumber and red onion. It's customary to start with a chicken satay, so you have an empty stick to skewer the cucumber and onions with, and dunk generously in peanut sauce.

SERVES 6

# Tea Leaf Eggs

These tea-infused eggs can be found in the most random places – from Chinese herbal shops, to *pasar malams* (makeshift markets), to your local 7-Eleven convenience store. Traditionally, hard-boiled eggs are left simmering in a large pot of tea, soy sauce and spices throughout the day. The intoxicating scent would draw the customers, and the eggs would be warm and ready to serve instantly. Unfortunately, that also means the egg whites turn rubbery and the yolks powdery. My version draws from the Japanese method of making ramen eggs. Instead of simmering the eggs, I marinate them for a day in the spiced brew. To create that beautiful classic marbled pattern, I leave the eggs unpeeled but gently crack the shells all over to allow the flavour and colour of the tea marinade to seep through.

750 ml (25 fl oz/3 cups) water, plus more to boil the eggs
2 black tea bags
4 tbsp dark soy sauce
4 tbsp light soy sauce
1 tbsp Shaoxing rice wine (optional)
1 tbsp light brown sugar
2 star anise
1 large cinnamon stick
thumb-sized piece (15 g/¼ in) fresh ginger, peeled and sliced
6 large free-range eggs, at room temperature

Let's start with the tea marinade. Bring the water to the boil and add the tea bags, soy sauces, rice wine (if using), sugar and spices. Cover and let simmer for 10 minutes, before straining and cooling completely.

Now for the eggs. Bring a large saucepan of water to the boil, enough to cover all the eggs in a single layer. Carefully lower the eggs into the boiling water one at a time. Turn the heat down to a medium–low so the water is at a gentle boil or an aggressive simmer. Cook for 6½ minutes, and when done, immediately transfer the eggs to a bowl of iced water to stop the eggs cooking.

When the eggs are completely cool to the touch, gently crack all over with the back of a spoon. You want to make enough cracks to allow the tea marinade to seep into the egg, but be gentle as the eggs are softer-cooked than the usual hard-boiled eggs. Transfer the eggs to a container and pour the tea marinade over, making sure they are all submerged. Refrigerate for a day for the flavours to infuse. The eggs will be good for up to 4 days in the fridge as the marinade helps to preserve them. The longer you leave them, the saltier and deeper the flavour and colour.

They can be served cold or warm – just gently warm the eggs in the marinade. When peeled, you should see a beautiful marble pattern all over the surface of the eggs.

# Kaya Toast with Half-Boiled Eggs

*Serves 2*

Whenever I go back to Singapore, my dad and I will find a quiet morning or afternoon to catch up, just the two of us, at a traditional kopitiam (coffee shop) nearby. Kaya toast is one of the few items served: white bread, toasted over charcoal, then slathered with a thick layer of pandan coconut jam. Slices of cold salted butter – generous enough to make the French blush – are then sandwiched in between the warm toasted bread and sweet kaya. It's the perfect contrast of flavours, textures and temperatures. But that's not all, for kaya toast is almost always served with 'half-boiled eggs' – eggs cooked so gently that the whites are custardy and the yolks are runny. You season the eggs to taste, mop it up with kaya toast, then wash it all down with a cup of strong coffee.

4 medium free-range eggs, at room temperature
4 slices of thin-sliced white bread
2–3 tbsp kaya (page 173)
½ cm (¼ in) slices from a block of cold, salted butter
dark soy sauce, to taste
ground white pepper, to taste

For the half-boiled eggs, bring a small saucepan of water to a rolling boil. The water should be deep enough to just submerge the eggs fully. Once boiling, remove from heat and gently lower the eggs into the water using a spoon, making sure they're in a single layer. Cover with a tight-fitting lid and leave aside for 6 minutes (see Note). Remove with a slotted spoon and rinse under cold running water to stop them cooking, then set aside.

For the kaya toast, cut the crusts off the bread and toast until golden brown. Slather each slice generously with kaya. Arrange the slabs of butter on two slices of bread, then cover with the remaining slices to form sandwiches. Cut each sandwich in half to get four rectangles.

To serve, tap the egg with the back of a spoon and break open carefully into a saucer, using your spoon to scoop every bit out. (You can't crack it open like a normal soft-boiled egg as the whites are so softly set.) Serve with the warm kaya toast on the side. Soy sauce and pepper are usually left on the table for people to help themselves to, so feel free to season the eggs to your liking.

Cooking times can vary by a minute or so, depending on the size of your pot and the thickness of the eggshells, so you may have to experiment in your kitchen! Have a spare egg to test. If the whites are still a little bit transparent, leave the remaining eggs for a minute longer. If it's perfectly cooked, you've got a bonus egg for the chef.

MAKES 2 × 200 ML (7 FL OZ/GENEROUS ¾ CUP) JARS

# Quick Kaya, aka Pandan Coconut Jam of Dreams

You can make this up to a week in advance, not just to spread on toast but for myriad puddings (see Pandan Swiss Roll, page 184). Traditional *kaya* is made by stirring whole eggs, coconut milk, sugar and pandan over very low heat for hours, until the mixture cooks and curdles. I shortcut this by using just egg yolks, much like you would when making lemon curd. The result is richer and smoother and, best of all, ready in minutes.

4 pandan leaves, cut into 3 cm (1¼ in) pieces
200 ml (7 fl oz/generous ¾ cup) coconut milk
100 g (3½ oz/½ cup) caster (superfine) sugar
4 free-range egg yolks
big pinch of fine sea salt

Blend the pandan leaves with half the coconut milk in a blender, then strain through a sieve (fine mesh strainer) to extract the green pandan juices. I like to mash the mixture in the sieve with the back of a spoon to make sure I squeeze every bit of flavour out before discarding the solids.

In a small saucepan set over medium heat, combine the pandan juice with the remaining coconut milk and the sugar and stir until dissolved. When the pandan is cooked, you'll see it turn brighter into a beautiful jade-green colour.

In a separate large bowl, beat the egg yolks. Slowly add a third of the pandan coconut milk into the bowl to temper the eggs, whisking all the time. Now pour the tempered egg mixture into the remaining coconut milk in the saucepan.

Cook for 15–20 minutes, stirring constantly until the mixture has thickened and coats the back of your spatula. Season with a pinch of salt, to taste. Then turn the heat down low and continue stirring until it gets to the consistency of thick custard. Transfer to jars – it will continue to thicken as it cools. Kaya is good for a week in the fridge, though I suspect you'll be finishing it off in days, with a spoon.

SERVES 3–4 AS A SNACK

# Sticky Kecap Manis and Lime Chicken Wings

**These chicken wings are the perfect party food – they are simple to make and a real joy to eat. You have to dig in with your hands, and you most certainly will have to lick the sweet, salty, sticky mess off your fingers after.**

4 tbsp kecap manis
juice of 1 lime (about 2 tbsp)
2 garlic cloves, grated
2 tbsp vegetable oil, plus more for greasing
¼ tsp fine sea salt
500 g (1 lb 2 oz) chicken wings
1 red bird's eye chilli, finely chopped
1 spring onion (scallion), finely chopped

Combine the kecap manis, lime juice and grated garlic, and divide the mixture among two bowls. In one bowl, stir together with the vegetable oil and salt, then pour this over the chicken wings, making sure they're evenly coated. Leave the chicken to marinate for at least an hour. To the other bowl, stir in the chopped chilli – this will form your dipping sauce later.

When ready to cook, preheat the oven to 200°C/180°C fan/400°F/gas mark 6. Drain the chicken, reserving the marinade. Lay the chicken wings out on a greased baking tray (pan) and roast in the oven for 20 minutes.

Flip the wings, brush with the reserved marinade and cook for another 10 minutes until browned and slightly charred.

Pour any pan juices into your dipping sauce and serve that alongside the chicken wings, garnished with the chopped spring onions.

MAKES 8–10

# Roti Jala, Turmeric Lacy Pancakes

These delicate Malay pancakes aren't served with fruit or maple syrup, they're the unlikely partner to a bold curry. I like to whip them up for dinner parties or when I have leftover curry, as they're easy enough to make and instantly elevate whatever dregs are left of a pot. Like British pancakes or crêpes, the batter is made with a few simple ingredients, but it's thinned out with coconut milk and dyed a glorious golden with turmeric. Traditionally, you would make *roti jala* by moving very quickly over a frying pan with… *a roti jala* mould, of course. It's a funny-looking object with multiple nozzles for the batter to flow freely from. Here, I just use a squeezy bottle to paint a net-like pattern in the pan.

100 g (3½ oz) plain (all-purpose) flour
¼ tsp ground turmeric
¼ tsp fine sea salt
1 large free-range egg
100 ml (3½ fl oz/scant ½ cup) coconut milk
about 100 ml (3½ fl oz/scant ½ cup) water
1 tsp vegetable oil, plus more for frying
salted butter, melted, for glazing (optional)

Blend all the ingredients, except the butter until you get a smooth batter with no lumps. Depending on how thick your coconut milk is, you may need to add an extra 2–3 tablespoons of water to adjust the consistency. You should aim for a runny crêpe-like batter. Let the batter rest for 15 minutes before pouring into a squeezy bottle.

To cook the pancakes, set a crêpe pan or small non-stick frying pan over medium heat and lightly grease the pan with a tiny amount of oil. Moving quickly, squeeze the batter all over the pan to create a net-like pattern. You can be methodical – horizontal lines, then vertical lines across the pan – or just go Jackson Pollock with it. Cook until the pancake is set, then brush with the melted butter (if using). You won't need to flip it since the pancake is so thin. Set aside on a large plate, with the glazed side facing down, then get going on the next pancake.

While I'm waiting for the next pancake, I do the folding. There are a couple of ways to do that: fold carefully in half into a half-moon shape and then again into quarters; or fold the sides in and then roll up gently into a spring-roll-like log. Loosely cover the tray of finished roti jala with a tea towel so they stay soft, while you finish up the batter.

Serve with any of the curries in the 'Curries' section (pages 45–62) and dunk generously into curry sauce.

SERVES 4

# Sweetcorn and Green Chilli Pakora

These spicy fritters have found their way from the streets of India to Singapore via the South Asian community, and are a firm local favourite. But rather than chai, I love my pakoras washed down with a cup of sweet frothy milk tea (*teh tarik*, page 196). I've also borrowed from the Malay cooks, who use rice flour for extra crispy *cucur* (fritters). My batter makes use of a mix of chickpea (gram) and rice flours, spiced with cumin, turmeric and hot green chillies. You can fry all sorts of vegetables in this versatile batter; here I've used tinned sweetcorn, a staple in many storecupboards.

1 small red onion, thinly sliced
½ tsp fine sea salt
325 g (11½ oz) tin sweetcorn (260 g/9 oz drained)
1–2 green bird's eye chillies, finely chopped (depending on spice preference)
small handful of fresh coriander (cilantro), finely chopped
1 tsp grated fresh ginger
½ tsp cumin seeds
¼ tsp ground turmeric
2–3 tbsp chickpea (gram) flour
2–3 tbsp rice flour
vegetable oil, for frying

TO SERVE

Coriander, Mint and Green Chilli Chutney (page 208)
Frothy Condensed Milk Tea (page 196) (optional)

Sprinkle the onions with half the salt and set aside – this will help them soften and release moisture. Meanwhile, drain and blitz the sweetcorn in a blender – pulse for a coarse texture, but make sure the corn kernels are all crushed, or else they may burst while frying.

Transfer the softened onions to a large mixing bowl, squeezing to release any liquid. Mix well with the sweetcorn, chillies, coriander, ginger and spices. Sprinkle the remaining salt and 2 tablespoons each of chickpea and rice flour and mix. You want to get a dough-like consistency, not a loose batter. If it's too soggy, add a tablespoon more of each flour.

Heat ½ cm (¼ in) of the oil in a wide frying pan over medium heat. You can check if the oil is hot enough by dropping a tiny bit of batter into it; it should sizzle immediately but not brown too quickly. Drop heaped tablespoons of the pakora mix into the pan, making sure not to overcrowd the pan. Leave undisturbed for a minute, before stirring gently to help the pakoras fry evenly. Once crisp and golden, remove with a slotted spoon onto a plate lined with kitchen paper (paper towels), while you fry the rest of the mixture.

If you aren't a fan of frying, you could spread out heaped tablespoons of pakora mix on a greased baking tray, then brush or spray them with oil, and bake at 180°C/160°C fan/350°F/gas mark 4 for 25–30 minutes; or in a greased air-fryer basket and cook at 180°C/350°F for 15 minutes, until golden.

While tempting to dig straight in, let them cool slightly or you'll burn the roof of your mouth off. Serve warm with the green chutney and, if you like, frothy condensed milk tea.

# SWEET

## CHAPTER EIGHT

# THINGS

CHAPTER EIGHT

# EIGHT

Growing up, dessert was usually a fat wedge of watermelon or pineapple. That doesn't mean we don't enjoy sweet things – in fact, we love them. In Singapore, we have sweet things at any time of the day, not just at the end of the meal.

On sluggish afternoons when you're after a pick-me-up, you might have tea and *kueh* – soft, chewy rice/tapioca/bean cakes flavoured with coconut and pandan, or delicate pancakes stuffed with sweet grated coconut or peanuts.

On hot, humid days, you might have tall towers of shaved ice, drenched in *gula melaka* (coconut palm sugar) syrup and topped with tapioca jellies. Or sweet iced shakes – fruit if you're being virtuous, a Milo Dino if you're not. I also have fond memories of the ice-cream cart parked just outside my primary school, touting *potong* ice cream (coconut popsicles) and made-to-order ice-cream sandwiches. The ice-cream man is a rare sight these days; in place of that we have new and exciting dessert shops – inspired by Italian gelaterias and French pâtisseries but flaunting creative local flavours like chrysanthemum tea, lemongrass and ginger.

Despite the weather, we also love our hot puddings. These tend to be a little bit more wholesome than their Western counterparts, being made with seeds, grains and pulses. You might get a black sesame paste – sesame seeds roasted until fragrant, ground until smooth and sweetened with rock sugar. Or *pulut hitam*, warm black sticky rice with coconut milk.

In this chapter, you'll find sweet things I grew up with, as well as new ideas that have inspired me for my supper clubs here. Serve them as dessert or do like a Singaporean would and enjoy them whenever you want.

SERVES 6–8

# Pandan Swiss Roll with Whipped Cream

I owe this Swiss roll recipe to my friend Cherry Tang. This is a friendship kindled, quite literally, over the stove. We met more than 10 years ago while London's supper club scene was growing, as each other's sous chefs/waiters/hungry guests. Today, she remains one of those I turn to regularly for advice – kitchen or life. Over lockdown, Cherry started making the most beautiful Swiss rolls – soft sponge cakes filled with whipped cream and strawberries, matcha sponges rolled with matcha custard cream, even delightfully purple ube ones. I'm not the most frequent baker, but spurred on by Cherry's lockdown bakes and seemingly everyone's banana breads, I made this pandan Swiss roll. I've adapted Cherry's perfect Swiss roll recipe with a smidge of pandan paste for that gorgeous green colour and fragrance, and filled it with cream and kaya (pandan coconut jam). You could squeeze pandan juice from fresh leaves, but in this case, I've found the ready-made extract to be not just easier, but a closer match to the pandan Swiss rolls of my childhood.

4 large free-range eggs, separated
80 g (3 oz) caster (superfine) sugar, divided
¼ tsp pandan extract paste
2 tbsp whole milk
pinch of fine sea salt
2 tbsp vegetable oil
50 g (1¾ oz/scant ½ cup) plain flour
1 tbsp cornflour (cornstarch)
dusting of icing (confectioner's) sugar, coconut flakes or fruit, to serve (optional)

### FOR THE FILLING

150 ml (5½ fl oz/scant ⅔ cup) double (heavy) cream, chilled
1½ tbsp gula melaka (coconut palm sugar) or light brown sugar
½ jar of kaya (pandan coconut jam) (page 173) (optional)

Line a 33 x 23 cm (13 x 9 in) Swiss roll baking tray with baking parchment (parchment paper) and preheat the oven to 180°C/160°C fan/350°F/gas mark 4.

Separate the eggs between two medium bowls and add 40 g (1½ oz) of sugar to each. Set the bowl with the yolks over hot water and beat with a whisk until doubled in size, pale and fluffy. Stir the pandan paste into the milk to dilute. Add the pandan milk, salt and oil to the bowl, sift the flours over, then whisk together until smooth.

As for the second bowl with the egg whites, whip into soft peaks using a hand whisk or electric beaters. Go slow if using electric beaters so you don't over whip! Gently fold the egg whites into the first bowl with a spatula, being careful to keep as much air as possible in the mixture. Start by spooning in a big dollop of the egg whites to loosen the mixture, then fold in the rest.

Pour the batter evenly into the baking tray, then lift and drop the tray onto the counter a couple of times to get rid of any air bubbles. Bake for 15–18 minutes until springy and dry to the touch and light golden.

When the sponge is ready, lift the edges of the baking parchment to transfer it onto a cooling rack. Five minutes later, when the cake has cooled slightly but is still warm to the touch, cover with a fresh sheet of baking parchment, and flip so the browned side is facing down. Peel the old baking parchment away and trim the edges of the sponge with a small bread knife to neaten. With the short edge of the sponge facing you, roll into a log. Leave it to cool completely, uncovered and rolled up like this, as this helps to prevent cracks later.

Meanwhile, in a chilled mixing bowl, whip the cream until it starts to form soft peaks. Add the sugar and keep whipping until you get stiff peaks and the cream doesn't flop over any more.

To assemble, unroll the sponge, spread an even layer of the kaya (if using) onto the cake, followed by the whipped cream. Roll again into a tight log, using the baking parchment underneath to wrap the cake up and twist the ends of the parchment to seal. Refrigerate for at least 2 hours to set.

To serve, unwrap and cut off the two ends of the roll before slicing it into rounds. You can finish this with a dusting of icing sugar, coconut flakes or fruit but it's delicious as is.

PAGE 184

PAGE 188

MAKES ABOUT 25

# Black Sesame Tang Yuan

*Tang yuan* are usually eaten during Lunar New Year reunions. All the children would be roped into helping the grown-ups roll tang yuan – if you could see above the table, you would be part of the crew. At its simplest, tang yuan is a sticky rice ball, made out of glutinous rice flour and water. Sometimes we would dye them in pinks and greens with drops of food colouring; other times we would stuff them with sweetened bean or seed pastes. Traditionally, lard would be added to the filling to give it a marvellous oozy, molten effect when you bite into it, but my version uses coconut oil for ease.

You can freeze the uncooked tang yuan, in a single layer, on a tray lined with baking paper (parchment paper). Once frozen, pop them into a freezer bag. They cook perfectly straight from frozen.

FOR THE GINGER SWEET SOUP

1 litre (34 fl oz/4¼ cups) water
a small knob of fresh ginger, peeled and sliced (about 30 g/1 oz)
100 g (3½ oz) light brown sugar, or to taste
2 pandan leaves, tied into knots (optional)

FOR THE BLACK SESAME TANG YUAN

100 g (3½ oz) black sesame seeds
3 tbsp light brown sugar
3 tbsp coconut oil, melted
pinch of fine sea salt
150 g (5½ oz) glutinous rice flour, plus extra for dusting
50 ml (2 fl oz) boiling hot water
75–100 ml (2½–3½ fl oz/ ⅓–scant ½ cup) room-temperature water, or as needed
black or white sesame seeds, to garnish (optional)

I like to get the sweet soup going first, as the longer you leave it, the more fragrant and spicy it gets. Bring all the ingredients for the sweet soup to a boil, then cover and turn the heat off while you prepare the tang yuan.

To make the black sesame filling, toast the sesame seeds in a dry frying pan, stirring often over medium heat. Needless to say, you can't quite tell by sight when the black sesame seeds are toasted, so you need to use your other senses – you will be able to smell their aroma, hear them popping in the pan. Then crush the dry, brittle seeds easily between your fingers. Let cool then blitz with the sugar and melted coconut oil until smooth. Let the mixture chill in the fridge for about 15 minutes so it firms up slightly, but isn't rock hard.

Once semi firm, scoop up about a teaspoon of the mixture and roll between your palms into a little black sesame ball. Repeat until you have used all the mixture. Set the black sesame balls aside on a tray in the fridge while you prepare your dough.

To make the tang yuan dough, add a pinch of salt to the flour in a large heatproof mixing bowl. Pour the boiling water over the flour, stirring in with a spatula. Slowly pour in the room-temperature water and mix with your hands until the dough comes together. You want to add the water bit by bit, as you might not need all of it! Knead until smooth, then let it rest, covered with cling film (plastic wrap) or a cloth, for 15 minutes.

This is a good time to gather the troops around the table. Roll out the dough onto a floured surface and cut into roughly 25 blobs. Flatten each piece between two floured palms, place the black sesame filling in the middle, then bring together the edges of the wrapper and press to seal, before rolling gently to smoothen. Don't panic if there are a few cracks – it's a very forgiving dough so just dab the crack with water and rub to reseal. Keep going until you finish, keeping the rest of the dough covered with a damp cloth so it doesn't dry out in the meantime.

Warm up the ginger sweet soup again. Bring a separate pot with plenty of water to a gentle boil over medium–high heat. Drop the tang yuan into the water and cook until they float to the top. Scoop into bowls with a slotted spoon and serve with the warm sweet soup. Garnish with a sprinkle of black or white sesame seeds if you like.

SERVES 5–6

# Black Sticky Rice Pudding with Rhubarb

*Pulut hitam* is heaven in a bowl – warm chewy grains of black glutinous rice, toffee-sweet with palm sugar and creamy coconut milk running through. But much like the best desserts, it can feel a little bit heavy, especially if you are having it at the end of a big meal. I adapted it for a supper club dessert by combining it with bright, sharp, poached pink rhubarb.

175 g (6 oz) black glutinous rice
100 ml (3½ fl oz/scant 1 cup) coconut milk
about 1 litre (34 fl oz/4¼ cups) water
1 pandan leaf, tied into a knot (optional)
¼ tsp fine sea salt, or to taste
75 g (2½ oz) gula melaka (coconut palm sugar), or to taste

FOR THE POACHED RHUBARB

100 g (3½ oz) rhubarb, cut into 2 cm (¾ in) pieces
10 g (¼ oz) caster (superfine) sugar
50 ml (2 fl oz/¼ cup) water

TO SERVE

100 ml (3½ fl oz/scant ½ cup) coconut milk
pinch of fine sea salt

Soak the black rice overnight in cold water. This helps the rice to cook more evenly and faster.

I also like to prepare the rhubarb the day before. Spread out the pieces in a single layer in a non-reactive frying pan and sprinkle with the sugar. Set aside for 15 minutes. Add the water and cook very gently, over very low heat, for a few minutes until it just starts to soften. Immediately turn the heat off and let cool. Then transfer into a container to chill in the fridge, making sure the rhubarb pieces are all submerged in the pink syrup.

The next day you'll see the black rice grains have absorbed the water and expanded. Drain, rinse and bring to a boil in a saucepan with coconut milk, the water and pandan leaf. Turn the heat down and simmer for another hour or, stirring once in a while, until the grains soften and break up, about 1 hour. You might need to top up with a bit more water as you go, though most of the liquid should be absorbed towards the end – you want to get to a thick porridge-like consistency. When it's done, season with the salt and gula melaka, tasting and adding more or less to your liking.

When you're ready to serve, in a separate small saucepan, warm the coconut milk with a pinch of salt. Scoop the black sticky rice into bowls and serve with the cold poached rhubarb and an extra drizzle of the warm coconut milk.

MAKES 5–6

# Pandan Pancakes Stuffed with Coconut and Palm Sugar

I have immense respect for the traditional Peranakan or Malay confectioners churning out assortments of light, colourful *kueh*. These sweet little bites often require complicated ratios of rice and bean flours, specific-shaped moulds, or multiple steps of steaming, resting and layering. *Kueh dadar* is one of the few that is easy enough to make. It's essentially a thin British pancake, but the batter makes use of coconut milk and fragrant pandan. Freshly shredded coconut, sweetened with *gula melaka*, is then stuffed into these light-green pancakes and rolled into delicate packets. As it's a hassle finding and then grating fresh coconut here in the UK, I've substituted desiccated (shredded) coconut moistened with a splash of coconut milk.

FOR THE SWEET COCONUT STUFFING

80 g (2¾ oz) desiccated (shredded) coconut
4 tbsp coconut milk
50 g (1¾ oz) gula melaka (coconut palm sugar)
¼ tsp fine sea salt

FOR THE PANCAKES

3 pandan leaves, roughly chopped (see Tip)
50 ml (1¾ fl oz/3½ tbsp) water
100 ml (3½ fl oz/scant ½ cup) coconut milk
1 large free-range egg, beaten
40 g (1½ oz/⅓ cup) plain (all-purpose) flour
1 tbsp caster (superfine) sugar
pinch of fine sea salt
1 tsp vegetable oil or melted coconut oil, plus more to fry

To make the stuffing, toast the coconut in a dry pan until light golden. Then stir in the coconut milk, gula melaka and salt. Cook for a few seconds until the coconut absorbs most of the liquid and is sticky and moist. Turn the heat off and set aside to cool.

Now let's make the pancake batter. If using fresh pandan, blend the leaves with the water and coconut milk, then strain through a fine sieve (fine mesh strainer) to extract the green pandan juice. I like to mash it in the sieve with the back of a spoon to make sure I squeeze every bit of flavour out, before discarding the solids. Add the egg and whisk to combine.

Separately, in a large bowl, combine the flour, sugar and salt and mix well. Pour the wet mix into the dry mix, whisking all the time until you get a smooth batter. The batter should be of a dripping consistency; if needed, thin out with a splash more coconut milk.

To make the pancakes, set a small non-stick frying pan over medium–low heat. Using kitchen paper (paper towels) or a brush, grease the surface of the pan with the tiniest amount of oil possible. Ladle the batter into the pan, swirling to cover the surface with a thin layer. The pancake should set in seconds and you *don't* want it to brown much. Transfer the cooked pancake to a tray and repeat until the batter is used up.

To assemble, scoop 2 tablespoons of coconut stuffing onto the middle of the pancake and spread it out horizontally, stopping 3 cm (1¼ in) clear from either side. Fold over the bottom half of the crêpe so that the filling is covered, then fold the sides in and roll into a parcel – it should look a bit like a spring roll! This is best made and served on the same day, but you can make the batter and stuffing ahead of time.

If you can't get hold of fresh or frozen pandan leaves, or just want a storecupboard shortcut, mix a scant ¼ teaspoon of pandan extract paste with the water and coconut milk. Too much turns the pancakes a lurid Halloween green.

SERVES 4

# Peach and Coconut Sago

Chilled 'sweet soups' are a common treat in Singapore's hot, humid weather. I'm especially fond of mango sago. This pudding was almost a guaranteed item on every Chinese wedding banquet menu in the 90s. As a little girl then, I didn't care much for the elaborate ceremony nor rare delicacies, but I always looked forward to this bright and refreshing end to the night. As mango sago is such a simple pudding, with few ingredients, it really relies on using the best-quality mango you can get. Save for a few Indian grocers during Alphonso mango season, a good mango is hard to come by in the UK, so I go for peaches instead, especially in summer. A peach that's ripe and in season has a honeyed sweetness and a perfume to rival that of a mango.

60 g (2 oz) sago (small white tapioca pearls)
4 ripe yellow-fleshed peaches
200 ml (7 fl oz/generous ¾ cup) coconut milk
2 tbsp sweetened condensed milk, or to taste (see Tip)
pinch of fine sea salt

Heat a pot with plenty of water over a high heat, and once it's at a rolling boil, tip in the sago. Turn the heat down and simmer for 15 minutes, stirring to prevent the sago sticking. The sago is cooked when it turns translucent; if there's still a white dot in the middle after 15 minutes, turn the heat off, cover the pot with a lid and let the sago sit in the hot water for another 10 minutes. Once cooked through, rinse the sago pearls through a sieve (fine mesh strainer) to remove excess starch, then drain and set aside in a bowl with plenty of cold water, until ready to use.

Set one peach aside for topping later, then peel, stone and roughly chop the remaining three. You should get about 200–250 g (7–9 oz) of chopped peaches. Blend the peaches in a blender with the coconut milk, condensed milk and a pinch of salt until smooth. Taste and adjust accordingly – depending on how sweet your peaches are, you might find you need to add a spoonful more of condensed milk. Transfer the peach and coconut mixture to the fridge to chill.

When ready to serve, drain the sago and fold into the peach and coconut mixture. Stone and cut the remaining peach, either into slices or cubes. I like to leave the skins on for their beautiful colours, so I don't peel here. Spoon the sago mixture into individual little bowls or glasses and top with the fresh cut peach. This is best served cold.

**TIP**

Tinned condensed milk is often used in Southeast Asian desserts to add a rich, syrupy sweetness. If you don't like it, or want to turn this vegan-friendly, you can replace it with caster (superfine) or coconut sugar, to taste.

SERVES 2

# Frothy Condensed Milk Tea

I had to include *teh tarik* in this section, as it's a true sip of Singapore. You might be thinking 'I know how to make tea', but *teh tarik* is a very different creature from English tea. We like our tea brewed very strong, steeped until it's deep and dark and bitter. Rather than a splash of fresh milk and an optional cube of sugar, we stir in condensed milk for an intense creamy sweetness. Now comes the fun part: we pour the milky tea between two steel jugs until it's frothy. As the tea is being poured, the jug will be raised higher and higher, so it will almost look like you're 'pulling' the tea ('*tarik*' means 'pulled' in Malay). This not only creates that famous froth, but it also cools the tea down to a perfect sip-ready temperature. It's the perfect bittersweet sidekick to any Singaporean meal, or on its own as a pick-me-up.

2 black tea bags (a strong one like Tetley or PG Tips)
250 ml (8 fl oz/1 cup) boiling water
2 tbsp condensed milk, or to taste

You'll need two little heatproof jugs or mugs to pour the tea between. Place the tea bags in one jug, pour the freshly boiled water over and leave to steep for at least 5 minutes until it's dark and strong.

Remove the tea bags, squeezing to get every last drop out, then stir in the condensed milk. Have a little taste and add more or less to your liking.

Hold the jug of milky tea in one hand and the empty jug in the other. Pour, trying to gain as much height as you can while you do so. Keep pouring back and forth until the tea is frothy.

Pour into cups and sip away immediately.

I'm well aware there are modern inventions like milk frothers or frothing whisks that pretty much do the same thing. Feel free to use them if you have them, but I promise the old-school method will be way more fun.

MAKES 10–12, DEPENDING ON SIZE OF YOUR ICE-LOLLY MOULDS

# Raspberry, Lime and Coconut Potong Ice Cream

This is one sweet treat that instantly takes me back to my childhood in Singapore. The ice-cream man came around not in a singing Mr Whippy van, but a freezer cart and giant umbrella set on wheels. Rather than soft serves or Cornettos, you had a choice of ice cream sandwiches, slabs of ice cream cut from a bigger block and stuffed into a slice of soft white bread; or potong ice cream – coconut ice lollies. I loved the latter. I would skimp at lunch breaks, saving up my coins instead for these cold treats. Potong ice cream came in a dizzying array of colours and flavours, made using local ingredients – sweetened red bean, purple yam or yellow sweetcorn. Here, I've used raspberries and lime to create a zesty, fruity, bright pink potong ice cream.

400 g (14 oz) fresh or frozen raspberries (see Tip)
400 ml (14 fl oz/1½ cups) tin of full-fat coconut milk
zest and juice (about 2 tbsp) of 1 lime
5 tbsp caster (superfine) sugar, or to taste

If you like, reserve a handful of raspberries to suspend in the finished lollies. Blend the remaining raspberries together with the rest of the ingredients until smooth. Taste and adjust accordingly – depending on how sweet or tart your berries are, you might find you need to add a touch more sugar.

If you have used fresh raspberries, let the mixture chill for a couple of hours in the fridge. If you used frozen raspberries, go right ahead to pour the mixture into the ice-lolly moulds, adding a few of the reserved raspberries now. They'll sink, so don't add them all at once! Freeze for an hour, then insert the lolly sticks and add the remaining reserved raspberries. Freeze overnight.

To remove your potong ice cream, dip the moulds in hot water for a few seconds, then carefully pull. Lick away, or if not eating immediately, wrap each one in baking parchment (parchment paper) and stick back into the freezer for those days when you want to feel like a child.

This recipe is incredibly versatile so feel free to vary with your favourite fruits. Try blueberries for a gorgeous purple ice cream, or peach or mango for a sunny yellow treat.

# SAUCES AND

## CHAPTER NINE

# SPRINKLES

**CHAPTER NINE**

# NINE

It's the extra bits that make a Singaporean dish really sing:

The rich sweet *sambal tumis* on a plate of *nasi lemak* (coconut rice).

The garlicky chilli sauce you dip (or drench) poached Hainanese chicken in.

The heavenly smell of fried shallots in a bowl of plain congee.

The sharp green pickled chillies you have in between each mouthful of fried *bee hoon* (rice vermicelli).

In this section, you'll find some of the most useful things to make lots of and to store in your fridge or pantry. Many of the recipes in this book call for these sauces and sprinkles, whether stirred into the wok at the start of a dish, or as the final flourish. Feel free to play with them in your own cooking to add spice, texture and/or fragrance.

# Sambal Tumis, Slow-Fried Chilli Sauce

MAKES ONE 200 ML (7 FL OZ/GENEROUS ¾ CUP) JAR

Sambal is the quintessential chilli sauce that's found on tables and menus across Singapore, Malaysia and Indonesia. There are hundreds of sambal recipes across the region, but this *sambal tumis* is my favourite of them all. 'Tumis' refers to the process of slowly frying the chilli paste until it caramelises and deepens in colour and flavour. It's good on pretty much anything and everything, not just the Singaporean dishes in this book. When I first started doing supper clubs, we would periodically release limited drops of my Red Hot Sambal Tumis. I would make only a dozen jars at once, post it onto our mailing list, and they would sell out in minutes. The anonymous sambal buyers would meet at a London tube station at a certain time and we would exchange the jars for a fiver. Years later, we make them in batches of 500 jars for Rempapa Spice Co. Below is a variation of that sambal.

10 dried red Kashmiri chillies
1 lemongrass stalk, base only, finely chopped
100 g (3½ oz) shallots, roughly chopped
2 garlic cloves
2 large fresh red chillies, roughly chopped
100 ml (3½ fl oz/scant ½ cup) vegetable oil
2 tbsp tamarind paste
½ tsp fine sea salt, or to taste
¾ tsp gula melaka (coconut palm sugar) or light brown sugar, to taste

Using kitchen scissors, roughly snip the dried red chillies and shake out the seeds. Soak in a bowl of hot water until soft, then drain. Pound the lemongrass, shallots, garlic, dried and fresh chillies together using a pestle and mortar or whizz in a small blender until you get a fine paste.

Heat the oil in a wok or deep frying pan set over medium heat. Once hot, add the chilli paste to the oil and turn the heat down to low. Fry the paste, stirring to make sure it doesn't stick or burn. It can take 30–45 minutes to cook, and if you're scaling the recipe up, it could take more than an hour. Use your senses to determine if it's ready – the chilli paste will darken to a deep red and you'll see the oil separating again from the mixture. It should smell very fragrant and have none of that 'raw' taste of shallots.

Stir in the tamarind, salt and sugar. Keep cooking until the sugar dissolves. Taste and adjust the seasoning as needed. Store in a clean jar in the fridge. The sambal will keep for up to 2 weeks if you make sure to keep it submerged under oil and not double dip.

MAKES ONE 200 ML (7 FL OZ/GENEROUS ¾ CUP) JAR

# Sambal Belacan, Shrimp Paste Chilli Sauce

What's unique about this chilli paste is belacan – fermented ground shrimp that comes in a pungent block. I still remember my British flatmates' faces changing the first time I cooked with it. Once toasted though, its fishy smell disappears and it adds an aromatic salty kick to this sambal – a must-have spicy accompaniment to most Nonya dishes.

1½ tbsp belacan (shrimp paste), roughly chopped or crumbled
8 large (200 g/7 oz) fresh red chillies, chopped (deseeded if you want it milder)
2 tsp light brown sugar, or to taste
zest and juice (4 tbsp) of 2 limes
½ tsp fine sea salt, or to taste

Open your windows. In a frying pan, toast the belacan over medium heat, pressing at it with your spatula to break it up. Stir-fry until hot, dry and powdery.

Pound the chillies, belacan and sugar together using a pestle and mortar until you get a fine paste, then stir in the lime juice and zest. If blending, just blend it all together.

Now taste and season with salt, as well as a touch more sugar if desired. I've suggested ½ teaspoon of salt here, but you might even find you don't need more than a pinch as different brands of belacan can be saltier than others.

MAKES ONE 200 ML
(7 FL OZ/GENEROUS ¾ CUP) JAR

# Garlic Chilli Sauce

This is another all-purpose chilli sauce it's worth making a jar (or two) of. I like to add a dollop onto snacks – particularly savoury kueh or anything crispy. It's also served as a dipping sauce for lots of Singaporean–Chinese dishes, like Teochew Braised Duck (page 75) and Hainanese Chicken Rice (page 132).

8 large (200 g/7 oz) fresh red chillies, chopped (deseeded if you want it milder)
5 garlic cloves, peeled
thumb-sized piece (15 g/½ oz) of fresh ginger, peeled
1 tbsp sea salt, or to taste
1 tbsp light brown sugar, or to taste
4 tbsp white rice vinegar or apple cider vinegar

Pound all the ingredients together using a pestle and mortar or whizz in a small blender until you get a fine paste. Taste and adjust seasoning as needed.

Store in a clean jar in the fridge. It will keep for up to a week if you take care not to double dip.

SERVES 2

# Chilli Padi and Soy Sauce Dip

This is the easiest dip you could possibly make – I say 'make', but really you are just bringing together two classic ingredients. We like to serve this alongside broths and noodle soups. Have a slurp and dip the broth-cooked vegetables or meat in this spicy and salty dip.

1 bird's eye chilli
2 tbsp light soy sauce

Finely slice the chilli and place in a little saucer. Stir in the soy sauce and serve.

This is so quick to pull together I rarely make this in advance, but it scales up easily and if you make a bigger batch it can be kept in a jar in the fridge for up to a week. Careful, it gets spicier the longer you leave it!

MAKES ONE 200 ML
(7 FL OZ/GENEROUS ¾ CUP) JAR

# Coriander, Mint and Green Chilli Chutney

This refreshing and fiery green chutney is often eaten alongside classic South Indian dishes like *thosais* or *pakoras* (see Sweetcorn and Green Chilli Pakora, page 178), but I love to serve this as a dip with all sorts of grilled or fried little bites.

¼ tsp cumin seeds
2 fresh green bird's eye chilies, chopped
1 tsp chopped fresh ginger
handful of fresh mint leaves (10 g/¼ oz)
bunch of fresh coriander (cilantro), (50 g/1¾ oz), leaves and stalks separated and roughly chopped
2 tbsp lime juice
2 tbsp plain yoghurt
½ tsp salt, or to taste
1 tsp sugar, or to taste
1–2 tbsp water

Toast the cumin seeds in a dry pan over medium heat until they smell really fragrant. Keep an eye on them and be careful not to overdo it as they taste bitter when burnt.

Set the coriander leaves aside, then blend all the other ingredients together in a blender, adding just enough water for it to come together into a chunky paste. Add the leaves and blend to a fine paste – don't over-blend as the heat causes the herbs to oxidise and darken. Taste and adjust the seasoning as needed.

This is best made and served on the day, but will keep in the fridge for 2 days in an airtight container.

SERVES 10
OR MAKES ONE 500 ML (17 FL OZ/2 CUPS) JAR

# Pickled Green Chillies

You will find this sharp fruity pickle served alongside all sorts of noodle dishes in Singapore, from *wonton mee* to fried *bee hoon* or *hor fun*.

6 large (150 g/5½ oz) green chillies
250 ml (8 fl oz/1 cup) white rice vinegar
1 tbsp caster (superfine) sugar
½ tsp fine sea salt

Thinly slice the green chillies and place into a clean glass jar.

In a saucepan, bring the vinegar, sugar and salt to a simmer, stirring to dissolve.

Pour the warm pickling liquid into the jar, making sure all the chillies are submerged.

Let cool completely before sealing and storing in the fridge. The pickle is ready the next day and will keep for 2 weeks in the fridge.

MAKES ABOUT 100 G (3½ OZ) FRIED SHALLOTS AND 250 ML (8 FL OZ/1 CUP) OIL

# Fried Shallots and Shallot Oil

You can buy tubs of fried shallots from most Asian supermarkets. They are handy to have in the larder for crispy garnishes. For the best flavour, it's worth frying your own. As a bonus, you get a fragrant oil that's infused with the heavenly smell of fried shallots.

100 g (3½ oz) shallots
pinch of fine sea salt
vegetable oil, for frying

Peel the shallots and slice thinly crosswise into rings. Just before you're ready to fry, sprinkle the shallots with salt. This helps them to crisp up more easily.

Heat about 1 cm (½ in) of oil in a wok or frying pan over medium heat. To test if the temperature is right, stick a wooden chopstick into the oil – you should see very tiny bubbles sizzling around it gently.

Add the shallots to the oil, spreading them out in a single layer. They should sizzle steadily. Fry for 8–10 minutes until the edges turn golden.

My trick is to turn the heat off at this stage and let the shallots continue to fry in the residual heat of the oil until they are perfectly golden.

Drain the fried shallots through a strainer set over a bowl. The shallots will crisp up and darken a bit more as they cool. Once cooled, transfer the fried shallots to an airtight container and shallot oil to a jar.

MAKES ABOUT 100 G (3½ OZ) FRIED GARLIC AND 250 ML (8 FL OZ/1 CUP) OIL

# Fried Garlic and Garlic Oil

Like the fried shallots, fried garlic is a wonderful final flourish to all sorts of Singaporean dishes. A sprinkle of fried garlic or drizzle of garlic oil instantly transforms light soups and plain steamed vegetables into something extraordinary.

1 garlic bulb
pinch of fine sea salt
vegetable oil, for frying

Peel and chop the garlic roughly. Just before you're ready to fry, toss the garlic with salt.

Heat about 1 cm (½ in) of oil in a wok or frying pan over medium heat. To test if the temperature is right, stick a wooden chopstick into the oil – you should see very tiny bubbles sizzling around it gently.

Add the garlic to the oil – it should sizzle steadily. Garlic burns a lot more easily than shallots, so you want to keep stirring as it fries.

When the garlic turns a very light golden, about 3–4 minutes, turn the heat off. Let the garlic continue to fry in the residual heat of the oil until perfectly golden.

Drain through a strainer set over a bowl. Once cooled, transfer the fried garlic to an airtight container and garlic oil to a jar.

MAKES ONE 200 ML (7 FL OZ/GENEROUS ¾ CUP) JAR

# Crispy Chilli Oil

I always have a jar or two of chilli oil in the fridge. I happily rotate among the traditional favourite Lao Gan Ma and the various small independent brands that have popped up recently in the UK. There are so many variations, but this is my go-to recipe when I'm making it at home. It's easy and delicious on everything – from congee to scrambled eggs to salads. Make sure to dig up the crispy bits.

3 tbsp dried red chilli (hot pepper) flakes
¼ tsp light brown sugar, or to taste
1 tsp fine sea salt, or to taste
175 ml (6 fl oz/generous ¾ cup) vegetable oil
8 garlic cloves, thinly sliced
1 star anise
1 cinnamon bark

Combine the chilli flakes, sugar and salt together in a jar.

In a small saucepan, combine the oil, garlic, star anise and cinnamon bark. Cook over medium–low heat until the garlic is light golden and crisp, about 10–15 minutes.

Remove the spices with chopsticks or a slotted spoon. Pour the garlic and oil over the chilli flakes and mix well.

Let cool before putting the lid on. The taste and colour of the chilli oil will deepen the longer it stands, so make it at least a day ahead. It will keep well in the fridge for up to a month.

MAKES TWO 1-LITRE (34 FL OZ/4¼ CUPS) KILNER JARS

# Second Auntie's Achar

All my Aunties have a signature dish that they bring to big family reunions. My Second Auntie is known as the achar maker of the family. This Peranakan pickle of vegetables, pineapple and roasted peanuts is an explosion of colour, taste and texture. Every bite gives you a different crunch and a different hit of sweet, sour or spicy. It's the perfect thing to go alongside coconut rice, rich meats and all sorts of Nonya braises and curries. I also often eat it straight from the jar. Below is an adaptation of her original recipe.

500 g (1 lb 2 oz) cucumber, seeds removed, cut into finger-length batons
200 g (7 oz) carrots, cut into finger-length batons
200 g (7 oz) cauliflower, broken into small florets
2 tbsp coarse sea salt
300 g (10½ oz) pineapple, peeled and cut into small pieces
100 g (3½ oz) white sesame seeds
200 g (7 oz) roasted peanuts

FOR THE PICKLING MARINADE

100 g (3½ oz) shallots
6 large (150 g/5½ oz) fresh red chillies, deseeded
1 tsp ground turmeric
100 ml (3½ fl oz/scant ½ cup) vegetable oil, for frying
125 ml (4 fl oz/½ cup) white rice vinegar, or white wine vinegar
150 g (5½ oz/⅔ cup) caster (superfine) sugar

Prepare the cucumber, carrots and cauliflower, toss with salt and set aside to sweat for 30 minutes.

Meanwhile, for the pickling marinade, pound the shallots, chilli and turmeric using a pestle and mortar or whizz in a small blender until you get a fine paste. Fry the spice paste in a pan over medium heat until aromatic, about 15 minutes. Have a taste – it shouldn't have any of that raw taste of shallots. Add the vinegar and sugar and bring to a simmer, then turn the heat off and let cool.

In a separate dry frying pan, toast the sesame seeds until golden, watching carefully to make sure they don't burn, and set aside to cool. Crush the roasted peanuts and combine with the sesame seeds.

Back to the vegetables. Drain any juices from the vegetables – the cucumbers especially will release quite a bit of moisture, so squeeze them as dry as you can. Combine with the pineapple pieces, sesame seeds and peanuts. Pour the pickling marinade over and mix well.

Transfer into glass jars, then seal and store in the fridge. It's ok if it looks like the vegetables aren't quite fully submerged in the pickling liquid, as they will continue to release their own juices as they pickle. The pickle is ready the next day and will last for 2 weeks in the fridge (if you can resist).

# ALTERNATIVE CONTENTS

## EASY FIRST-TIMER RECIPES

Oyster Sauce Sweetheart Cabbage  87

Hot Smoked Mackerel and Ginger Congee  156

Fried Egg Tempra with Onions and Kecap Manis  102

Mum's Soy Braised Pork Belly and Shiitake Mushrooms  76

Sticky Kecap Manis and Lime Chicken Wings  174

Green Beans with Turmeric and Toasted Coconut  91

## PARTY PERFECT

8-hour Ox Cheek Rendang  48

Salt and Pepper Crispy Roast Pork Belly  111

Peranakan Prawn and Pineapple Curry  52

Steamed Aubergines with Cherry Tomato Sambal  122

Roti Jala, Turmeric Lacy Pancakes  176

Black Sticky Rice Pudding with Rhubarb  190

## WHEN THE SUN IS SHINING

BBQ Chicken Satay with Tamarind Peanut Sauce  166

Cucumber, Pineapple and Peanut Rojak with Tamarind Dressing  92

Lime-cured Fish with Chilli Padi and Pink Onions  120

Steamed Mussels with Coconut and Laksa Leaves  116

Peach and Coconut Sago  194

Raspberry, Lime & Coconut Potong Ice Cream  198

## FAIL-SAFE FAMILY FAVOURITES

Chilli Crab Spaghetti 141

Childhood Wonton Mee 144

Clay Pot Rice with Shiitake and Chinese Sausage 154

Vegetables and Tofu Puffs in Coconut Milk 54

Hainanese Chicken Rice 132

Black Sesame Tang Yuan 188

## SUPER-SPEEDY

Fish Sauce Omelette 100

Nasi Goreng 142

Shu's Spicy Late Night Special 96

Rainbow Chard Belacan 88

Drunken La La with Rice Wine 118

Steamed Egg Custard 98

## FLAVOUR-PACKED VEGAN

Silken Tofu with Salted Black Beans and Spring Onion 105

Kam Heong Fried Cauliflower 124

Mamak Lentil Dal with Fried Curry Leaves 58

Roast Pumpkin Masak Lemak 56

Char Bee Hoon with Wild Garlic and Fried Tofu 150

Pandan Pancakes Stuffed with Coconut and Palm Sugar 192

(There are many more recipes in the book which are vegan or come with vegan options, so take this list as a starting point!)

## ABOUT THE AUTHOR

Shu Han Lee grew up in Singapore and moved to London in 2009. Author of the acclaimed Chicken and Rice, Shu is a recipe developer whose sauce company, Rempapa Spice Co., is stocked throughout the UK, including in Selfridges and Whole Foods.

## THANK YOU

To my family, for sharing their love of food with me. No journey or queue was ever too long for the best fishball noodles, and I owe the stories and ideas in this book to our collective gastronomic 'research' over the years. To my Mum, for also sharing her love of cooking with me. The thousands of meals you have cooked for the family have inspired my own journey as a cook and many of the recipes in this book. To my husband Olly, for all the taste-testing, idea-bouncing, dish-washing and everything else in between.

To the Hardie Grant team: Kajal, for 'sliding into my DMs' with the message that started it all in the first place! Eve and Issy, my commissioning editors, for having faith in me and whipping my ideas into shape with so much energy and enthusiasm. Eila, for her patience in getting us from drafts and proofs to a real, tangible cookbook. And Helena for the meticulous copy editing to make every recipe read well. It has been an absolute joy writing this book thanks to all of you.

To the shoot team: Sam, for bringing my recipes to life and making every drop of sauce/ strand of noodle look glorious. Louise and Kristine, for assisting and barely breaking a sweat at the never-ending list of rempah prep. Ola, for photographing every dish so beautifully and always being up for 'one more shot, maybe with hands?' Martyna, for providing said hands, and role-switching from hand model to assistant photographer to in-house barista with cheer. Louie, for hunting down the plates and fabrics of my dreams and being the creative mastermind behind each set.

To the incredibly talented Evi O and team: Susan, Katherine, Emi, Matt and Doreen, for transforming my scrappy mood board and rambling thoughts into this magnificent thing. You have captured the colour and spirit of Singapore so wonderfully in these pages.

To my agent Emily, for being there every step of the way, and for lending me your wisdom and your kitchen over the past ten (ten?!) years.

To all those who contributed recipes, thoughts and ideas in any way: my second aunt Angela Ang, for her achar recipe – handwritten, photographed and sent over WhatsApp without a moment's hesitation. Cherry Tang, for her Swiss roll recipe and patience as my long-distance baking teacher. Christopher Tan, for his thoughtful insight into 'agak agak' and Singaporean cooking. And the generations of Singaporean cooks and chefs who have gone before me.

To all the people who have visited my supper clubs, or bought a Rempapa jar or two, or cooked from my books and recipes. I wouldn't have been able to do what I do without your support and encouragement. All your feedback and ideas over the years have helped me to become a better cook and to learn how to finesse these recipes to work for everyone.

This book wouldn't have been possible without you, and I hope you all love it as much as I do x

# INDEX

## A

ACHAR
    second Auntie's achar 212
ASPARAGUS
    steamed asparagus with garlicky black bean sauce 94
AUBERGINES
    steamed aubergines with cherry tomato sambal 122

## B

BEANSPROUTS
    char bee hoon with wild garlic and fried tofu 150–1
    Katong curry laksa 136–7
    Uncle's 'dry' laksa 138
BELACAN
    rainbow chard belacan 88
    sambal belacan, shrimp paste chilli sauce 205
BLACK BEANS
    silken tofu with salted black beans and spring onion 105
    steamed asparagus with garlicky black bean sauce 94
BLACK SESAME SEEDS
    black sesame tang yuan 188–9
BRAISES 67
    braised egg tofu with mushrooms and sugar snaps 80–1
    chicken braised in tamarind and coriander 79
    Mum's soy-braised pork belly and shiitake mushrooms 76
    Teochew braised duck with sweet soy and galangal 75
BROCCOLI
    childhood wonton mee 144
BROTHS 67
    basic stock (broth) 69
    chicken or pork stock 69
    vegetarian stock 69

## C

CABBAGE
    oyster sauce sweetheart cabbage 87
    vegetables and tofu puffs in coconut milk 54
CARROTS
    ABC sweetcorn, carrot and pork rib soup 74
    vegetables and tofu puffs in coconut milk 54
CAULIFLOWER
    kam heong fried cauliflower 124
CHICKEN
    BBQ chicken satay with tamarind peanut sauce 166
    chicken braised in tamarind and coriander 79
    chicken in red sauce 45
    chicken or pork stock 69
    Hainanese chicken rice 132–3
    lime leaf chicken curry 46
    Nonya lemongrass roast chicken 115
    soto ayam with spring greens 70
    sticky kecap manis and lime chicken wings 174
CHILLIES
    chicken in red sauce 45
    chilli padi and soy sauce dip 206
    coriander, mint and green chilli chutney 208
    crispy chilli oil 210
    garlic chilli sauce 206
    pickled green chillies 208
    sambal belacan, shrimp paste chilli sauce 205
    sambal tumis, slow-fried chilli sauce 204
    sweetcorn and green chilli pakora 178
CHUTNEY
    coriander, mint and green chilli chutney 208
CLAMS
    drunken la la with rice wine 118

COCONUT, DESICCATED
  fresh herb rice salad 34
  green beans with turmeric
    and toasted coconut 91
  pandan pancakes stuffed with
    coconut and palm sugar 192–3
COCONUT MILK
  8-hour ox cheek rendang 48
  black sticky rice pudding
    with rhubarb 190
  coconut rice 33
  pandan pancakes stuffed with
    coconut and palm sugar 192–3
  peach and coconut sago 194
  quick kaya, aka pandan coconut
    jam of dreams 173
  raspberry, lime and coconut
    potong ice cream 198
  roast pumpkin masak lemak 56
  roti jala, turmeric lacy
    pancakes 176
  steamed mussels with coconut
    and laksa leaves 116
  vegetables and tofu puffs
    in coconut milk 54
  yellow sticky rice 38
CONDENSED MILK
  frothy condensed milk tea 196
CONGEE
  hot smoked mackerel
    and ginger congee 156
  plain congee 36
CORIANDER
  chicken braised in tamarind
    and coriander 79
  coriander, mint and green
    chilli chutney 208
CRAB
  chilli crab spaghetti 141
CREAM
  pandan swiss roll
    with whipped cream 184–7
CUCUMBER
  cucumber, pineapple and peanut
    rojak with tamarind dressing 92
  second Auntie's achar 212
CURRIES 43
  8-hour ox cheek rendang 48
  Assam fish, runner bean
    and tomato curry 51
  chicken in red sauce 45

Hainanese pork and new potato curry 47
lime leaf chicken curry 46
Mamak lentil dal with
  fried curry leaves 58
Peranakan prawn
  and pineapple curry 52
roast pumpkin masak lemak 56
Tamil egg curry 62
vegetables and tofu puffs
  in coconut milk 54
CURRY LEAVES
  cereal prawns with butter
    and curry leaves 112
  Mamak lentil dal
    with fried curry leaves 58
CUSTARD
  steamed egg custard 98

# D

DAL
  Mamak lentil dal
    with fried curry leaves 58
DUCK
  Teochew braised duck with
    sweet soy and galangal 75
DUMPLINGS. *SEE WONTON DUMPLINGS*

# E

EGGS
  braised egg tofu with mushrooms
    and sugar snaps 80–1
  fish sauce omelette 100
  fried egg tempra with onions
    and kecap manis 102
  hot smoked mackerel
    and ginger congee 156
  kaya toast with half-boiled eggs 170
  nasi goreng 142
  steamed egg custard 98
  Tamil egg curry 62
  tea leaf eggs 169
  Teochew braised duck
    with sweet soy and galangal 75
  torn noodles with poached egg
    and watercress 158

## F

FISH
Assam fish, runner bean
  and tomato curry 51
hot smoked mackerel
  and ginger congee 156
lime-cured fish with
  chilli padi and pink onions 120
Teochew steamed fish with pickled
  mustard greens 117
fish sauce omelette 100

## G

GALANGAL
Teochew braised duck with
  sweet soy and galangal 75
GARLIC
fried garlic and garlic oil 209
garlic chilli sauce 206
steamed asparagus with garlicky
  black bean sauce 94
GINGER
black sesame tang yuan 188–9
hot smoked mackerel and ginger
  congee 156
meatball soup with lettuce
  and fried ginger 72
GREEN BEANS
green beans with turmeric
  and toasted coconut 91
nasi goreng 142
vegetables and tofu puffs
  in coconut milk 54

## H

HAKE
Assam fish, runner bean
  and tomato curry 51
HERBS
fresh herb rice salad 34

## I

ICE CREAM
raspberry, lime and coconut
  potong ice cream 198

## K

KAYA
kaya toast with
  half-boiled eggs 170
quick kaya, aka pandan coconut
  jam of dreams 173
KECAP MANIS
fried egg tempra with onions
  and kecap manis 102
sticky kecap manis and lime
  chicken wings 174
KETCHUP
soy sauce and ketchup prawns 86

## L

LAKSA LEAVES
steamed mussels with coconut
  and laksa leaves 116
LEMONGRASS
Nonya lemongrass
  roast chicken 115
LENTILS
Mamak lentil dal with fried
  curry leaves 58
LETTUCE
meatball soup with lettuce
  and fried ginger 72
LIME JUICE
lime-cured fish with chilli padi
  and pink onions 120
sticky kecap manis and lime
  chicken wings 174
LIME LEAVES
lime leaf chicken curry 46

## M

**MACKEREL**
    hot smoked mackerel and ginger congee 156

**MEATBALLS**
    five-spice ngoh hiang meatballs 164
    meatball soup with lettuce and fried ginger 72

**MUSHROOMS**
    braised egg tofu with mushrooms and sugar snaps 80–1
    char bee hoon with wild garlic and fried tofu 150–1
    clay pot rice with shiitake and Chinese sausage 154
    Mum's soy-braised pork belly and shiitake mushrooms 76
    Mum's steamed pumpkin rice 153

**MUSSELS**
    steamed mussels with coconut and laksa leaves 116

**MUSTARD GREENS**
    Teochew steamed fish with pickled mustard greens 117

## N

**NOODLES**
    char bee hoon with wild garlic and fried tofu 150–1
    childhood wonton mee 144
    Katong curry laksa 136–7
    torn noodles with poached egg and watercress 158
    Uncle's 'dry' laksa 138

## O

**OATS**
    cereal prawns with butter and curry leaves 112

**OIL**
    crispy chilli oil 210
    fried shallots and shallot oil 209

**OMELETTE**
    fish sauce omelette 100

**ONIONS**
    fried egg tempra with onions and kecap manis 102
    lime-cured fish with chilli padi and pink onions 120

**OX CHEEK**
    8-hour ox cheek rendang 48

**OYSTER SAUCE**
    oyster sauce sweetheart cabbage 87

## P

**PAKORA**
    sweetcorn and green chilli pakora 178

**PANCAKES**
    pandan pancakes stuffed with coconut and palm sugar 192–3
    roti jala, turmeric lacy pancakes 176

**PANDAN LEAVES**
    pandan jasmine rice 32
    pandan swiss roll with whipped cream 184–7
    quick kaya, aka pandan coconut jam of dreams 173

peach and coconut sago 194

**PEANUTS**
    BBQ chicken satay with tamarind peanut sauce 166
    cucumber, pineapple and peanut rojak with tamarind dressing 92
    second Auntie's achar 212

**PEAS**
    Shu's spicy late night special 06

**PICKLES**
    pickled green chillies 208
    second Auntie's achar 212

**PINEAPPLE**
    cucumber, pineapple and peanut rojak with tamarind dressing 92
    Peranakan prawn and pineapple curry 52
    second Auntie's achar 212

PORK
- ABC sweetcorn, carrot and pork rib soup 74
- chicken or pork stock 69
- classic pork and prawn filling [dumplings] 146
- five-spice ngoh hiang meatballs 164
- Hainanese pork and new potato curry 47
- meatball soup with lettuce and fried ginger 72
- Mum's soy-braised pork belly and shiitake mushrooms 76
- salt and pepper crispy roast pork belly 111
- Shu's spicy late night special 96
- torn noodles with poached egg and watercress 158

POTATOES
- Hainanese pork and new potato curry 47

PRAWNS
- cereal prawns with butter and curry leaves 112
- classic pork and prawn filling [dumplings] 146
- five-spice ngoh hiang meatballs 164
- Katong curry laksa 136-7
- Peranakan prawn and pineapple curry 52
- soy sauce and ketchup prawns 86
- Uncle's 'dry' laksa 138

PUMPKIN
- Mum's steamed pumpkin rice 153
- roast pumpkin masak lemak 56

# R

rainbow chard belacan 88

RASPBERRIES
- raspberry, lime and coconut potong ice cream 198

RHUBARB
- black sticky rice pudding with rhubarb 190

RICE 29-30
- black sticky rice pudding with rhubarb 190
- clay pot rice with shiitake and Chinese sausage 154
- coconut rice 33
- fresh herb rice salad 34
- Hainanese chicken rice 132-3
- Mum's steamed pumpkin rice 153
- nasi goreng 142
- pandan jasmine rice 32
- plain congee 36
- steamed fragrant sticky rice 37
- yellow sticky rice 38

RICE BALLS
- black sesame tang yuan 188-9

RICE WINE
- drunken la la with rice wine 118

RUNNER BEANS
- Assam fish, runner bean and tomato curry 51

# S

SAGO
- peach and coconut sago 194

SALADS
- fresh herb rice salad 34

SAUCES
- garlic chilli sauce 206
- sambal belacan, shrimp paste chilli sauce 205
- sambal tumis, slow-fried chilli sauce 204

SAUSAGE
- clay pot rice with shiitake and Chinese sausage 154

SHALLOTS
- fried shallots and shallot oil 209

SHRIMP
- Mum's steamed pumpkin rice 153
- rainbow chard belacan 88

SHRIMP PASTE
- sambal belacan, shrimp paste chilli sauce 205

SOUP
- ABC sweetcorn, carrot and pork rib soup 74
- Katong curry laksa 136-7
- meatball soup with lettuce and fried ginger 72
- soto ayam with spring greens 70

SOY SAUCE
    chilli padi and soy sauce dip 206
    soy sauce and ketchup prawns 86
    Teochew braised duck with sweet soy and galangal 75
SPAGHETTI
    chilli crab spaghetti 141
SPRING GREENS
    soto ayam with spring greens 70
SPRING ONIONS
    silken tofu with salted black beans and spring onion 105
STOCK
    basic stock (broth) 69
    plain congee 36
    vegetarian stock 69
STOCK CUBES 69
SUGAR SNAP PEAS
    braised egg tofu with mushrooms and sugar snaps 80-1
SWEETCORN
    ABC sweetcorn, carrot and pork rib soup 74
    sweetcorn and green chilli pakora 178
SWISS ROLL
    pandan swiss roll with whipped cream 184-7

# T

TAMARIND
    BBQ chicken satay with tamarind peanut sauce 166
    chicken braised in tamarind and coriander 79
    cucumber, pineapple and peanut rojak with tamarind dressing 92
TANG YUAN
    black sesame tang yuan 188-9
TEA
    frothy condensed milk tea 196
    tea leaf eggs 169
TOFU
    braised egg tofu with mushrooms and sugar snaps 80-1
    char bee hoon with wild garlic and fried tofu 150-1
    Katong curry laksa 136-7
    silken tofu with salted black beans and spring onion 105
    tofu, fried leek and carrot filling [dumplings] 146
    vegetables and tofu puffs in coconut milk 54
TOMATOES
    Assam fish, runner bean and tomato curry 51
    chicken in red sauce 45
    chilli crab spaghetti 141
    steamed aubergines with cherry tomato sambal 122
    Teochew steamed fish with pickled mustard greens 117
TURMERIC
    green beans with turmeric and toasted coconut 91
    roti jala, turmeric lacy pancakes 176
    yellow sticky rice 38

# V

VEGETABLES
    second Auntie's achar 212
    tofu, fried leek and carrot filling [dumplings] 146
    vegetables and tofu puffs in coconut milk 54
    vegetarian stock 69

# W

WATER CHESTNUTS
    five-spice ngoh hiang meatballs 164
WATERCRESS
    torn noodles with poached egg and watercress 158
WONTON DUMPLINGS 146-9
    childhood wonton mee 144

Published in 2024
by Hardie Grant Books,
an imprint of Hardie
Grant Publishing

Hardie Grant Books (London)
5th & 6th Floors
52–54 Southwark Street
London SE1 1UN
Hardie Grant Books (Melbourne)
Building 1, 658 Church Street
Richmond, Victoria 3121

hardiegrantbooks.com

All rights reserved. No part of this publication may be reproduced, stored in a retrieval system or transmitted in any form by any means, electronic, mechanical, photocopying, recording or otherwise, without the prior written permission of the publishers and copyright holders.

The moral rights of the author have been asserted.

Text © Shu Han Lee

Photography © Ola O. Smit

Photography on pages 10, 11, 12, 28, 42, 50, 60–61, 66, 68, 84, 108, 130, 162, 172, 182 and 202 © Shu Han Lee

Illustrations © Evi-O.Studio

British Library Cataloguing-in-Publication Data. A catalogue record for this book is available from the British Library.

Agak Agak
ISBN: 978-1-78488-666-0

10 9 8 7 6 5 4 3 2 1

**PUBLISHING DIRECTOR**
Kajal Mistry

**COMMISSIONING EDITOR**
Eve Marleau

**PROJECT EDITORS**
Isabel Gonzalez-Prendergast and Eila Purvis

**DESIGN & ART DIRECTION**
Evi-O.Studio | Susan Le

**TYPESETTING**
Evi-O.Studio | Matt Crawford & Doreen Zheng

**ILLUSTRATIONS**
Evi-O.Studio | Katherine Zhang & Emi Chiba

**PHOTOGRAPHER**
Ola O. Smit

**FOOD STYLIST**
Sam Dixon

**PROP STYLIST**
Louie Waller

**COPY-EDITOR**
Helena Caldon

**PROOFREADER**
Esme Curtis

**INDEXER**
Cathy Heath

**PRODUCTION CONTROLLER**
Martina Georgieva

Colour reproduction by p2d
Printed and bound in China by Leo Paper Products Ltd.